POISONOUS POWER

JOSEPH MATTERA

Cultivating Healthy Influence in an Age of Toxic Leadership

Copyright © 2023, 2019 – by Joseph Mattera

Publisher—Mattera Media
Brooklyn, New York

All rights reserved. This book is protected by the copyright laws of the United States of America. This book may not be copied or reprinted for commercial gain or profit. The use of short quotations or occasional page copying for personal or group study is permitted and encouraged. Permission for other usages must be obtained from the author. Scriptures marked NASB are taken from the NEW AMERICAN STANDARD BIBLE®, Copyright © 1960,1962, 1963,1968,1971,1972,1973,1975,1977,1995 by The Lockman Foundation. Used by permission. Scripture quotations marked ESV are from the ESV® Bible (The Holy Bible, English Standard Version®), copyright © 2001 by Crossway, a publishing ministry of Good News Publishers. Used by permission. All rights reserved.

ISBN: 979-8-9864582-8-1 Paperback
       979-8-9864582-9-8 eBook

CONTENTS

FOREWORD 5
INTRODUCTION 9

PART 1: PREPARED FOR PASTORAL LEADERSHIP
1. THE RITES OF PASSAGE TO GOD-GIVEN INFLUENCE 13
2. SIGNIFICANT QUESTIONS TO ASK BEFORE BECOMING A LEAD PASTOR 19
3. COMMON MISTAKES PASTORS MAKE..25
4. YOUNG LEADERS: LOOK BEFORE YOU LEAP....................................35
5. LEADING REASONS PASTORS FALL (AND SOLUTIONS) 39
6. HOW FAILURE CAN EMPOWER SUCCESS 51
7. WOULD THE APOSTLE PAUL BE CONSIDERED A SUCCESS TODAY?........61
8. BUILDING EMPIRES BUT NOT GOD'S KINGDOM..............................67
9. THE KINDS OF PEOPLE NOBODY CAN HELP 75

PART II: PROBLEMS IN LEADERSHIP
10. BIBLICAL STANDARDS FOR LEADERSHIP IN AN AGE OF SCANDAL 83
11. WARNING SIGNS BEFORE LEADERSHIP FAILURE 95
12. SIGNS OF POWER-HUNGRY LEADERS 101
13. SIGNS OF ABUSIVE LEADERSHIP 107
14. LESSONS LEARNED FROM HIGHLY-PUBLICIZED FALLS 113
15. WHAT CHURCHES CAN LEARN FROM OTHERS IMPLODING 119
16. SIGNS OF LEADERSHIP BURNOUT..125
17. THE GREATEST TEMPTATIONS FOR LEADERS IN THE WILDERNESS 131
18. CHARACTERISTICS OF DEMIGOD LEADERS 137
19. HOW THE MIGHTY FALL 147
20. THE SEVEN DYSFUNCTIONS OF AN ORGANIZATION 153

PART III: GUIDELINES FOR THE LONG HAUL
21. THE SINS AND TEMPTATIONS OF YOUNG, MIDDLE-AGED, AND OLD LEADERS 159
22. WHAT WE CAN LEARN FROM MICHAEL JACKSON'S TRAGEDY 165
23. WAYS PREACHING CAN HURT MORE THAN HELP........................177
24. THE CHALLENGES AWAITING EXECUTIVE LEVEL LEADERS........181
25. AVOIDING THE LEADING REGRETS OF AN 80-YEAR-OLD MINISTER 189
26. SIGNS OF AUTHENTIC LEADERS 195
27. LEADERSHIP PRINCIPLES FOR FINISHING WELL........................201

CONCLUSION 207

FOREWORD

There is an increasing awareness in the last few decades of the challenges that are posed when the darker side of power is present in various settings amongst leaders, including church leaders. The various behaviors associated with such abuses of power are legion and make news headlines frequently. The challenge we face as followers of Christ is not only how to deal with such blatant misuses and abuses of "power," rather the issue of "when" such issues are addressed is equally problematic.

More often than not, the environment that such leaders create in order for followers to embrace the kinds of corruption and exploitation that take place make those environments conducive for repeated offenses, silence, and covering up. There is a conditioning psychologically that forms and shapes what enables leaders to misuse their position of influence, violate trust, and abuse power.

Within the academic and practitioner world of organizational leadership such issues have been and are being researched and examined with great rigor. Sadly, within far too many organizational structures in both independent local church movements and denominational settings, such research and examination isn't taking place, or if it does take place it is always after the fact, when remedial efforts have to be taken to bring corrections and adjustments not just to the leaders, rather also to the environments they have created and the followers they have subjugated.

The lust for power is as old as the fall of man, and the excuses made by those who are toxic in their use of power are equally ancient. The real challenge is that from a Christological perspective, we are without excuse. To justify claiming a kind of grace that enables one to make an excuse for the abuse of power, as for example in the life of David, is to ignore what has taken place in the context of the New Covenant by virtue of the incarnation, the death, the burial, the resurrection, and the ascension of Christ and the outpouring of the Holy Spirit who now indwells those who believe.

We are currently "bent" on an approach to justification that seems to completely ignore the issues of sanctification that are equally essential in a life lived in Christ with genuine internal integrity. Far from an "Old Testament" sermon, the Sermon on the Mount indeed is the Magna Carta of life in Christ. The issues Jesus covers there leave us little wiggle room for compromise and excuse-making, because they are rooted in total and absolute dependence on Christ Himself to indwell us.

Our theological presuppositions are flawed because our cultural accommodations to fit in have compromised our faithfulness to the Son, the Spirit, and the Scriptures, "the Father's three-fold cord" that Leonard Sweet argues cannot be separated without damage and detriment to our lives and to the Church at large.

Joseph Mattera is a Biblical scholar. His academic rigor however does not preclude his intimacy in his relationship with the Triune God. In actual fact, it is his intimacy with the Father, through the fellowship of the Son by the power of the Spirit that informs his scholarship when it comes to the sacred text. His concerns about the dark side of leadership are not a mere castigation of the evident behaviors amongst church leaders that indeed are toxic. Rather, Joseph understands the times in which we live, and draws deeply from the ancient wells of the Christian Tradition with a capital "T", and calls us soberly forward to once again come to terms with the way in which the Father, the Son, and the Spirit actually lead us.

If we place Jesus side-by-side with the great "leadership gurus" of the Western world, his approach to dealing with fellow human beings in a one-on-one setting, or in small groups, or larger gatherings, or in the ecclesia itself would offer a profound challenge to the Western models of leadership that are rooted far more in ancient Greek and Roman culture and bear no resemblance whatsoever to what Paul says when he utters the words of Jesus as part of his approach to leadership: "Follow me, as I follow Christ." There is only One who can say, "Follow Me," without the tinge or marring of toxicity. The rest of us would be wise to apply the dictum of Paul and invite others to follow us insofar and only as far as we ourselves are actively, intimately, intentionally, and deliberately following Jesus.

Thanks Joseph for *Poisonous Power*. It is a wake-up call to genuine self-awareness, self-reflection, and self-examination for every generation of leaders in the Body of Christ in the day and the hour in which we live. Your admonitions are much needed and I pray they will be much heeded.

Bishop Mark J. Chironna
Church On The Living Edge
Mark Chironna Ministries
Longwood, Florida

INTRODUCTION

Too often, church leaders make headlines for the wrong reasons. This book emerged from a series of essays I wrote in recent years addressing the nature of, challenges in, and biblical solutions for church and marketplace leadership. My observations stem from nearly four decades of ministry in the church, community, and marketplace as an activist, mentor, and cultural exegete. (Often, leaders have to function like a cultural anthropologist who analyzes and understands human endeavor and behavior in order to navigate through sociological, psychological, and geo/political complexities to accomplish their goals.)

I have organized the chapters of this book into three sections, starting with some essentials those seeking to lead a church need to acquire and a review of common mistakes. Part II is the longest section, reflecting the signs of our times when it comes to misguided, abusive, or power-hungry leaders. I conclude on a hopeful note, reviewing some guidelines for long-term success in ministry—and life.

In order to be successful, we need to learn to recognize successes and failures, strengths and weaknesses, and functional and dysfunctional leadership styles and methodologies. My prayer is that these writings will aid both accomplished and emerging leaders to develop more self-awareness so they will hit the bullseye of their calling in life.

Above all, may this work advance gospel movements by inspiring, educating, and equipping Christ-centered leaders—the kind of leaders who will make Christ's body shine brightly instead of bringing disgrace to His name.

—*Joseph Mattera*

PART 1: PREPARED FOR PASTORAL LEADERSHIP

CHAPTER 1

THE RITES OF PASSAGE TO GOD-GIVEN INFLUENCE

"And Jesus, full of the Holy Spirit, returned from the Jordan and was led by the Spirit in the wilderness" (Luke 4:1, ESV).

I HAVE BEEN INVOLVED in full-time church ministry since 1980, and have observed leaders go through many phases as they shift from one stage to another. In this chapter I am calling these phases "rites of passage"—or ROP. I use this term to refer to a person's transition from one place to another, based on their ability to pass a series of challenges. In the church we have various ceremonies that mark different phases of spiritual and biological maturity, such as baptism, first Communion, and confirmation. However, in the context of this chapter, a rite of passage is more a test and part of a process God uses to bring believers into another stage of maturity before assigning them to another level of Kingdom service.

Biblically, we see great leaders who have gone through different stages of their lives. These tests prepared them for something greater than what they were initially called to do. For example, the patriarch Joseph, one of the sons of Jacob, had various tests and experiences before God elevated him to second-in-charge to the Pharaoh in Egypt. Moses was in the wilderness for 40 years before God called him to be the deliverer of Israel. King Saul persecuted David, who hid in the wilderness for many years before David became the king of Israel. Even Jesus was in the wilderness for 40 days, being tested by Satan before He began His public ministry. Jesus also had to endure agony in the Garden of Gethsemane before He was ready to go to the cross and be raised from the dead.

The following are some ROPs that I see as necessary in progressing in ministry:

1. Dependence on God instead of man

The higher your calling, the greater the tests and more intense ROP you will have to go through. As we look at the most effective leaders in the Bible, they all had one thing in common: their utter dependence on God to fulfill their callings. The more you grow into your higher calling, the more fragility you will experience, along with so many moving parts that you must trust God to bring everything together every day so you can survive. This is the only kind of person He can release to the highest levels of spiritual leadership. Jesus taught us to ask the Father for "our daily bread" (Luke 11:2-4), which has to do with daily spiritual, emotional, and physical provision—not just financial.

2. Learning courage in the face of fear

One thing I learned many years ago was that obedience to the will of God meant that I had to leave a predictable life in order to live a life of risk, based on faith. You live on the edge so much and in so many areas that it sometimes takes courage just to climb out of bed in the morning. God cultivates courage during an intense ROP in our lives to prepare us for our next Kingdom assignment.

3. Obscurity

One of the greatest ROP is a willingness to obey God without earning the accolades of men. God cannot thrust us into the public eye if we cannot first serve Him faithfully in obscurity. For example, Jesus was hidden for at least thirty years before He began His public ministry (Luke 3:23), and John the Baptist was approximately the same age as Jesus when he emerged from the wilderness to preach and prepare the way of the Lord (Luke 3:1-9).

4. Adversarial circumstances

One of the most common ROP occurs during times of testing, where everything in our lives is under attack. I have had seasons in my life, lasting more than several years at a time, in which I experienced major pushback and conflict in every area of my personal life and ministry. I knew this was my ROP because it always came right before God wanted to bring me into another level of my divine assignment.

5. Financial lack

Sometimes there is no immediate provision for a divine vision. God uses these times to test our hearts to see if we want to do something for Him based on financial gain, or for His glory. He also wants to know if we will continue to move forward in obedience, even if we do not see a long-term financial solution. For instance, the children of Israel were required to continue to obey God, even when they did not know where their next meal was coming from when they wandered in the wilderness for 40 years.

6. Silence from heaven

There are times of testing in which, for long periods of time, we do not receive clear words of affirmation or confirmation regarding a calling from God that He gave us a long time ago.

It is always much easier to keep on going when we receive ongoing prophetic encouragement and/or divine endorsements through others. But maturity and preparation are often cultivated more inside of us when the heavens are silent for a period of time, when we have to live completely by faith (Isaiah 42:19).

7. Loving those who hurt and abuse us

One of the hardest ROP is during times when you experience relational conflicts and misunderstandings with those closest to you. This is a crucial lesson that involves learning how to love unconditionally through the insults, abuse, neglect, and persecution. If God can trust us to walk in forgiveness and love the unlovely unconditionally, then He can trust us to demonstrate His heart to others in higher levels of leadership, no matter what the circumstance or response.

Truly, being a Christ follower necessitates a high level of emotional maturity as per the teachings of Jesus as shown in what is known as the "Lord's Prayer" that teaches us to forgive the debts of others as well as the "Sermon on the Mount"that teaches us to love those who mistreat us (Luke 11:2-4 and Matthew 5-7).

8. Faithfulness during the mundane

It is probably much easier to demonstrate faithfulness to God when there are big events, a crisis, and/or great movement, replete with incessant action. I believe more people fall into unfaithfulness when things get boring and mundane. This is a key ROP that teaches the believer to cultivate the joy of the Lord during slow, boring days and seasons in their lives. Consider Moses being 40 years in the wilderness of Midian. That prepared Him for the last 40 years of his life, which featured non-stop action as he became the deliverer of Israel. (See the Apostle Paul's admonition to the church in 1 Thessalonians 4:11, 12.)

9. Finding contentment only in God

Ultimately, the greatest ROP is to learn to get ultimate satisfaction in honoring and worshiping Him. Every person and everything we have or accomplish in this life will soon pass away, and God will often work to strip out of our hearts every secondary thing we depend on for happiness and fulfillment. God releases His highest calling to those who delight themselves in Him (Psalm 37:4).

10. Prioritizing our mission and focus

Finally, one of the greatest rites of passage for accomplished leaders is the ability to say, "No" to good opportunities and open doors. God will often test us to see what we will say, "No" to before he brings better opportunities He wants us to say, "Yes" to.

In closing, I pray that this chapter will help you recognize the season of life you are in and the ROP you may be going through at the present time. As you contemplate the crises you may be in, it may also be time to consider some questions I raise in the next chapter—especially if you aspire to a greater position of responsibility.

CHAPTER 2

SIGNIFICANT QUESTIONS TO ASK BEFORE BECOMING A LEAD PASTOR

As we all know by now, thousands of lead pastors leave full-time church ministry every year. Along those same lines, a high percentage of new church plants never make it past three years! One reason is that most potential lead pastors never honestly attempt to ask themselves the following questions:

1. Am I emotionally mature enough to take on myself the rigors of taking the lead role in a church?

Whether it is a new church plant or taking over the lead role from another pastor, a lead pastor has to be emotionally mature enough to deal with the incredible emotional challenges of the ministry.

Lead pastors must have thick skin. They cannot hold grudges against people. They have to learn how to forgive those who betray them, break covenant, and handle adversity and crisis. It is not enough to know how to preach well. Emotional maturity is perhaps even more important than having a good personality and giftedness in the pulpit!

2. Am I theologically competent?

Most new pastors, especially of the independent evangelical/Pentecostal ilk, have inadequate formal theological training. Before you venture into a lead pastorate, make sure you have enough theological depth to be able to feed the flock of God 52 weeks per year. Pastors cannot get by just on preaching evangelistic messages or their pet doctrinal passions. They have to learn how to expound on the whole counsel of God (Acts 20:27)!

In recent decades, there have been many successful pastors who have come out of a marketplace background. Unfortunately, most of them lead the church more like the CEO of a secular corporation than as a shepherd of the flock of God. Having business acumen and administration is necessary, but administration without theological depth produces a church that has great marketing and impressive crowds and programs, but superficial disciples.

3. Am I organizationally competent?

Being theologically trained is not enough. I have found that most pastors have no clue in regard to formulating a church budget and administration. It doesn't matter how anointed you are or how good a preacher you are! Administration is needed to harness the anointing and create systems in the church for the proper implementation of church vision.

To illustrate this point, God created natural laws within complex systems and framed the physical world before He placed living creatures and humanity on the earth (Genesis 1). Hence, there was an organized, systemic foundation before there was human activity.

4. Is my spouse emotionally and spiritually prepared for such a task?

Many go into the pastorate without weighing the toll it will take on their spouses and children. I have found that the wife of a male lead pastor is one of the neediest people in the body of Christ. Many have never been adequately prepared for the high demands people will place on their lives and families. These spouses should expect that people in the congregation will want to visit their home, call whenever they are in need, and expect them to drop everything when they have an emergency. People in the congregation expect the wife of the lead pastor to function as the "mother" of the church and will get offended if the spouse does not give them adequate attention!

God calls a couple into the pastorate, not just one-half of the marriage. (Also, I do not generally believe it is a good idea for single people to enter into the pastorate, since they will be faced with numerous sexual temptations, especially from other needy single people who want their counsel and oversight.)

5. How do I know that God is calling me into the pastorate?

Perhaps the most important question a potential lead pastor can ask himself or herself is this: "Did God really give me this assignment?" When the trials and stresses related to church ministry come their way, they will seriously consider abandoning the pastorate if they are unsure of their divine calling.

6. Do I have in place sufficient mentors who can walk with me and gauge my progress?

Every lead pastor should have several mentors in their life. Not only do they need other seasoned and successful lead pastors, but they will need mentors regarding their psychological health, finances, physical health, and legal advice in setting up a proper board of elders, trustees, by-laws, and ongoing minutes. These mentors should have a trusting relationship with the lead pastor and be allowed to speak honestly into their life, or else it will be a waste of time for both parties. (Paul's legacy letters to Titus and Timothy are examples of the incredible value of having a mentor guiding young leaders through the arduous task of doing the work of the ministry.)

7. Do I have a sufficient support system of peer relationships and friends?

Every leader learns quickly that it can get lonely at the top! Lead pastors desperately need a constellation of other godly peers in the ministry and a tight-knit social community they can relax with, and pray with, who are not always talking about the challenges of the ministry. Lead pastors need a regular mental break from the rigors of ministry, and they cannot do it alone.

8. Have I taken the time to meet with the other lead pastors in my region to get advice?

If I had to do it all over again, I would have met with and obtained advice from every cooperative lead pastor in my community before I planted our church. They would have been able to give me the lay of the land, share their experiences related to the specific challenges of that region, and become potential friends and a part of my support system in the ministry!

(About eight years after our initial church plant, I started a monthly pastors' covenant support group with about 12 local area pastors, which became an incredible source of unity and strength for us all.)

9. Do I have a proper business plan for financial sustenance?

The old Pentecostal adage was to just obey the calling of God and trust God for the finances. Of course, that is the primary foundation. But, having a proper business plan for the church is absolutely necessary in this complicated world, one fraught with financial scandal, strict IRS regulations, and enormous complexities regarding present economic realities.

10. Do I have a proper philosophy of ministry that matches my calling and personality?

Every lead pastor has a different personality, gift mix, and method of ministry. Pastoring a church should never be done using a cookie-cutter approach that mimics other successful leaders. Lead pastors who attempt to lead just like one of their ministry heroes are usually headed for failure and/or great disappointment. There is only one you; every leader is unique and must flow properly in their gift mix in order to be effective!

Some helpful questions to start off with include these: What is my personality type? (Am I an introvert or extrovert?) What are my motivational gifts? (Romans 12:4-8.) What manifestations of the Spirit usually accompany my ministry? (1 Corinthians 12:4-8.) What fivefold ministry function do I operate in? (Ephesians 4:11)

In closing, I wish someone had given me some advice like this in the late 1970s, before I got married and entered full-time church ministry. It would have saved me a lot of unnecessary heartache and trauma! Forewarned, I would have been forearmed when it comes to avoiding some of the common mistakes pastors make, the subject of chapter 3.

CHAPTER 3

COMMON MISTAKES PASTORS MAKE

As a pastor for over 35 years, I have learned much through the School of Hard Knocks. My goal in this chapter is to identify some of the most common mistakes made by pastors and leaders, so others coming in their footsteps will not replicate them.

1. They try to disciple their congregation solely from their pulpit messages

I learned a long time ago that often no more than half the congregation is paying attention and attempting to retain all that you teach. One of the ways I compensate for this is to encourage everyone to write notes while I teach; only 10 percent of what you preach will be remembered the next day by those in the congregation who fail to take notes.

In addition, approximately one-third of most congregations is missing on any given Sunday. Thus, discipleship is greatly limited. One way to compensate is for the pastor to regularly teach a series of messages that build on one another with a quick review of the previous lesson, thus allowing those who missed the previous week to stay in the flow and learn. However, as important as congregational preaching is, the most effective way to disciple and train believers is by teaching them in small groups and in informal mentoring as Paul instructed Timothy (2 Timothy 2:2).

I frequently meet with a small group of about 10-12 men that I pray with, teach, and share my heart with. Also, I often take a few people with me when I travel and minister so we can spend time together, which gives them time to learn my ways, not just hear me preach on Sunday.

2. They think vision trumps the culture of the church

Leaders often believe that presenting a mission statement to the congregation is enough to create momentum and move the church toward its goals.

However, before a leader can implement a new vision, the culture of a church has to change. For example, if a church is going to adopt a cell church strategy, their old program-based culture (mindsets, habits, ways) will first have to change through one-on-one meetings with key people. It will also take months of prayer, strategy, implementation, and—most importantly—having all the key leaders and members of the church or organization successfully implementing cell groups as their main focus (in regard to evangelism, training leaders, and actualizing the mission) before they attempt to get the rest of the congregation to walk in it.

3. They invest most of their time nurturing people instead of developing leaders

The main difference between pastors and apostolic leaders is that pastors spend all their time visiting and nurturing all the sheep, while apostolic leaders focus 80 percent of their time with the 20 percent of the congregation who will produce

80 percent of the ministry. When lead pastors spend most of their time nurturing those who lack the potential to be leaders, they limit the growth of the congregation and become the bottleneck to expansion.

4. They place people in ministry based on giftings instead of integrity and character

The foundation of our life is our character, not our giftings. Thus, if we place people in a ministry function before the foundation of their character is deep enough, we are posturing our church to be a personality and gift-driven entity that doesn't have what it takes to enjoy its current rate of success beyond 3-5 years. The general rule of thumb is that a person will be able to walk in their purpose when their gifting and anointing to minister are commensurate with integrity and godliness. When a person's gifts and abilities exceed the level of their spiritual and emotional maturity, huge problems will follow.

5. They fail to communicate adequately with their spouse and key leaders before making big decisions

This sets the senior leader up for marital problems and/or disconnect or division among the key leaders of the organization. Through the years, I have seen this happen more than once; indeed, I have made important announcements and as I was making them, observed an astonished look on my wife's face! The point is this: Even if you have a great idea, the pastor should always give their spouse and primary leadership time to "buy in" to all major decisions before announcing them.

6. They spend more time in administration than in study and prayer

Many pastors I know are functioning as glorified deacons, who focus more on marketing and administration than on seeking God in the secret place.

God has called for pastors to be "kings and priests," not just to serve as kings! The priestly function allows the kingly function to hit the mark in regard to decisions and impact.

Acts 6:2-4 clearly teaches that the senior leader's primary function is prayer and the ministry of the Word. Those who focus on this, as well as developing leaders and delegating administration to their disciples, will flourish most in regard to their primary purpose.

7. They fail to put up boundaries to protect their family life

Many pastors' wives blame the ministry for 80 percent of their marital problems. I know of many pastors who allow congregants to call their homes, interrupt family time or dinnertime, or allow visitors to stop by at all hours of the night, thinking this is what God expects of them. This is probably the single biggest reason why children of preachers hate the ministry and would never think of imitating their parent's faith and works.

This is one reason why I counsel pastors to have an office OUTSIDE of their home—to keep set office hours and separate church work from their family time in regard to their focus.

Without setting proper boundaries, the pastor will inevitably sacrifice their family on the altar of ministry, alienating both spouse and children.

8. They feel threatened by other gifted and strong leaders instead of harnessing them

Insecure leaders limit the ministry capacity of strong, emerging leaders instead of harnessing and then releasing them to their destiny. Having a large church does not necessarily mean a church is successfully developing and releasing emerging leaders to their destiny.

Insecure pastors and leaders will always have cycles of division in their churches because they frustrate those with mantles of leadership on their lives by not making room for their gifts. The results of unfairly capping potential leaders is either splitting congregations or organizations, starting a new church or entity prematurely, or having these leaders attending other churches as they look for greener pastures. Churches with a history of church splits and divisions may have an insecure senior pastor who needs to become emotionally whole before the church can release mature sons and daughters into the harvest field.

9. They try to have success without a successor

Some pastors I know are well into their 60s and still don't know who their successor will be! Often, the spouse of the pastor takes over after the senior leader passes away, thus thrusting a person who is likely uncalled and unqualified into an executive leadership position. Other leaders just put one of their children in as the new leader, even though there is clear consensus among the primary leaders that this person is not yet ready—or even called.

Regarding our priorities as leaders, the moment we step into any ministry we should begin to work ourselves out of a job by training others to do the work of the ministry (Ephesians 4:11-12). One rule of thumb for senior leaders is to delegate everything others can do almost as well as they can, while only focusing on things no one else is qualified to do.

10. They fail to understand the three components of vision: hindsight, insight, and foresight

A leader cannot successfully take their organization into the future if they don't learn from the past and accurately interpret the present.

11. They fail to affirm those working for and with them

Ninety percent of all the feedback human beings receive regarding themselves is negative. This issue is so important even Jesus didn't go forth to minister until He received affirmation from His Father (Luke 3:22). Senior leaders should regularly affirm those who faithfully serve in their organization. Affirmation releases people to their destiny like nothing else!

Unfortunately, often times pastors replace fatherly affirmation and affection with the laying on of hands. But the laying on of hands is only supposed to be the culminating seal of a long-term process of nurture, love, and relationship building that are the foundation of properly releasing ministers and workers to their destiny.

12. They never adequately develop accountable peer relationships among other ministers

Every leader needs three levels of relationships:

1. Spiritual children
2. Brothers and sisters (peer relationships)
3. Spiritual parents (every pastor needs a pastor)

Not having accountable level two and three relationships leaves a leader vulnerable to their own sinful tendencies, which can shipwreck everything they have ever worked for. A pastor who doesn't have an overseeing pastor or bishop is already in error!

13. They fail to bring their children along as part of their ministry team

Merely placing our children in Sunday school one hour per week is not as good as having them serving as part of your ministry. Have them come along with you on mission trips and hospital visitations or to prayer meetings releases them to minister with you in the church. Getting them involved with children's choir, evangelistic teams, skits and other evangelistic activities allows your children to take ownership of the ministry instead of making them feel like they are merely being dragged along against their will. If the latter happens, as soon as they are old enough (when they have a choice) they will leave both the church and the ministry!

14. They attempt to develop faithful members instead of sons and daughters

The greatest title I have by far in our church is the title "Dad." A church or ministry will only be effective to the extent it has developed the army of God out of the family of God! Having a lot of laborers without a spirit of sonship results in merely having a house of slaves or servants. Sons will always be more loyal than servants because sons are assured of their father's love, their placement and role in the house, and their share of the inheritance.

15. They go by the latest Christian contemporary fads instead of building on proven biblical principles

I have some minister friends who change the vision of their church every few years, based on the latest renewal movements or strategies featured on the covers of Christian magazines. Although we can learn much from what God is doing in other parts of the world, we need to know our core values and purpose, and build everything else around this. When a church changes its vision too often, the senior leader loses credibility, and the congregation senses instability.

16. They fail to be transparent with their inner circle and congregation

Senior leaders who share with their inner circle their internal and personal struggles pave the way for more transparency and trust among their core leadership. To a certain extent, even sharing personal challenges from the pulpit can actually encourage folks in the congregation because they feel more of a sense of trust and connection with the leader; they also feel encouraged, knowing that they are not the only ones struggling in their Christian life and faith.

17. They fail to utilize the principles of Matthew 18:15-18

In our church, we have made walking in the light a staple and core value. This is because I have found that communication between leadership eradicates 98 percent of all potential problems and cuts off Satan's game of deception and accusation.

For years, I made it a requirement for those serving with me in leadership to receive Communion together and promise to walk in the principles of Matthew 18:15-18. Those failing to make this vow were asked to step down until they were willing to comply. I refuse to work with people who can't promise that they will come directly to my wife or me or another team member in cases of offense. The reason for this is because experience tells me that offense is inevitable among those who work the closest together. Those not walking in the light are a train wreck waiting to happen!

18. They fail to get their congregation to take ownership of the vision and they develop employees instead of proprietors

Employees check in at 9 a.m. and clock out at 5 p.m., even if there is an emergency and more work is needed. In contrast, a proprietor clocks in early and leaves only when the work is done. Even if it is 5 p.m., if a pipe breaks in the basement of their business, they will stay until midnight to make sure it is fixed, long after employees have left for the day. All effective organizations successfully transfer ownership of the vision to their adherents, who are shareholders of the organization.

19. They preach individual blessing and destiny instead of the biblical model of corporate blessing

The typical preaching in America is about individual destiny instead of corporate purpose. This is the case in spite of the fact that 95 percent of the Bible was written to either the nation of Israel or the body of Christ.

A person can't "write their own ticket" with God if they are not flowing with the corporate destiny of their local church. Our historical faith teaches us that it is never just us and God, or just an individual and their Bible. Second Peter 1:20 teaches that Scripture is never about one's own private interpretation.

For example, our fingers need a hand, which needs an arm, which is connected to a shoulder, etc., in order to function properly!

All biblical prophecies are corporate; there is no such thing as an individual prophecy because all biblical examples were either to the nation of Israel or to the church, or they were for an individual regarding their ministry to Israel or the body of Christ.

20. They build one-generational instead of multi-generational works

God revealed Himself to Moses as the God of Abraham, Isaac, and Jacob, and has called us to think strategically for at least three generations in everything that we do.

Most leaders act as though God is just the God of Abraham, since they focus only on their present lifetime. I tell leaders all the time that if they reach their highest purpose and potential while they are alive, they have failed miserably because Scripture teaches that those who follow in our footsteps should do greater works than we have done (John 14:12; Psalm 78:1-4).

21. They glibly say, God "spoke" to them and lose credibility when it doesn't happen

I tell leaders never to say, "Thus saith the Lord," when they either attempt to prophesy or speak out what they feel God has spoken regarding their church or organization.

If you say, "The Lord said," then you already preclude judging the word, because who can judge God? We should always say, "I believe the Lord is saying," because everyone's prophetic words are subjective and should be scrutinized by the counsel of core leadership. I have seen many pastors and leaders glibly say the Lord has spoken to them and then not long afterwards the Lord told them something else. (Of course this is after the word didn't come to pass!) I have especially seen this when a leader says that God promised them a building for the church or a similar proclamation. When a leader speaks out like this, they begin to lose credibility with their congregation; then, the next time they speak no one will listen!

Now that I have reviewed a rather long list of pastors' common mistakes, let's move on to examine seven mistakes young leaders often make.

CHAPTER 4

YOUNG LEADERS: LOOK BEFORE YOU LEAP

As a person who started off in full-time ministry at the ripe old age of 21, I write the following out of personal experience and not only observation. We desperately need young leaders to emerge! We older leaders need to help them come forth! That being said, these are some common mistakes young leaders make that can hinder their progress. The following are seven of the top mistakes young leaders make:

1. Young leaders often have zeal without knowledge

Perhaps the greatest attribute of young leaders can also be their greatest weakness: zeal. The Bible tells us it is possible to have zeal (great energy and passion) without knowledge

(Romans 10:2). This can manifest in having great excitement and motivation to accomplish a great task. And yet, in that excitement, still overlook many of the necessary details needed to ensure success. Such leaders can see the forest but fail to see the individual trees that make up the forest.

2. Young leaders often neglect the advice of older, wiser leaders

Like Rehoboam (1 Kings 12), the son of Solomon, young leaders often surround themselves with like-minded leaders their own age and neglect the advice of older, more seasoned leaders. Perhaps this is because the next generation thinks they understand contemporary culture better than older leaders, or perhaps this stems from a generation gap. Whatever the reason, young leaders make huge mistakes (as did King Rehoboam) if they attempt to lead without the advice and accountability of more experienced leaders.

3. Young leaders often put their work before their families

All young leaders struggle with having balance in this area. One of the main reasons is because young people have an intense need to prove their competency and accomplish great things to satisfy their egos and lift their self-esteem. Consequently, this intense desire often blinds them to the needs of their families, which often leads to emotionally neglecting their spouses and children.

If this is not rectified quickly enough, the foundations of their families will be faulty and they may have huge issues in the future. Older ministers have learned that it doesn't pay to win the world and lose their families!

4. Young leaders often compete with, instead of partner with, other leaders

Along with an inordinate desire to prove themselves comes an intense, subconscious drive to be more successful than other leaders their own age. (Even pastors fall into this trap.) Young leaders need to learn not to compare themselves with their peers since they all have unique gifts and callings others cannot easily replicate (2 Corinthians 10:12). They also need to understand how partnering with other like-minded leaders will actually maximize their ability to get things done for the sake of the Kingdom!

5. Young leaders have unrealistic goals

Often young leaders believe they will be able to see quick results and bring incredible transformation overnight. Their goals are often unrealistic and idealistic. This recalls the words of an old rabbi: "When I was young I wanted to change the world. When I got a little older, I modified my goals and wanted to change my nation. Then, as I got older, I was content to merely change my city. Then my community. Now that I am very old, I would just like to change myself!"

Although I do believe God can use a young person to change their nation and/or the world (D. L. Moody, Billy Graham, John Wesley, Charles Finney, George Whitefield, or Dr. Martin Luther King, Jr., are examples.), for the most part young leaders have to avoid being precocious regarding their goals and be more practical in regard to following a process capable of facilitating their vision.

6. Young leaders lack biblical balance regarding truth

Often young leaders are focused on one area of truth that gives them passion, to the neglect of other areas of their lives. For example, young senior pastors may focus on one subject, such as prosperity, healing, deliverance, or evangelism, but if they neglect other truths of the Bible they will build unbalanced congregations. Young leaders need to study the whole counsel of God and not just areas based on their passions.

7. Young leaders often build without a proper foundation

Often young leaders will build a business or even plant a church without taking the time needed to build a proper foundation. Whether it is having a strong leadership team in place or a plan for sustainable growth, young leaders often put the cart before the horse and may even experience immediate success, but without long-term fruit. The deeper the roots of a tree grow into the ground, the taller the tree can grow!

In the beginning, young leaders need to take more time building a proper foundation than being concerned about how quickly they can make money and/or grow their businesses or ministries.

No matter what your age, pastors sometimes experience emotional meltdowns or falter before reaching a ripe old age in ministry. In chapter 5, I will review some of the reasons ministers fall apart.

CHAPTER 5

LEADING REASONS PASTORS FALL (AND SOLUTIONS)

(Some of the ideas in this chapter come from insights shared by Linda Lindquist-Bishop, during an email exchange.)

Through the years I have often analyzed why so many pastors fall into sin or resign from church ministry. I came up with a number of primary reasons, which are enumerated in this chapter.

1. Churches are becoming complex enterprises, which some pastors are not equipped to lead

The typical seminary training one receives to be a pastor usually only slightly touches on the practical elements needed to oversee a church in the 21st century. Learning theology and how to exegete Scripture is not enough. Pastors have perhaps the toughest job in the nation.

The following are some of the issues contemporary pastors grapple with:

Real Estate: Pastors must deal with zoning laws; political leaders; community boards; and bank, business, and community leaders.

Many churches of a thousand or more are larger than the average church often because of location; so much of the mega-church phenomenon is based on sociological/geographical reasons, not just anointing, gifting, and how much prayer takes place.

Like a McDonald's franchise, one of the most important keys to success is not the quality of a ministry, but its location. In other words, are there ample options for parking and/or is the facility near public transportation; is the facility visible to the masses of people; are there other considerations? Thus, pastors need to have skill in picking out the right location.

New Facility: Pastors must hire the right architect, lawyer, and other consultants to organize a grueling capital stewardship campaign. These campaigns are enough to destroy many churches because the pressure of fundraising can easily become the focus, instead of ministering to the needs of the people.

Cash Flow Questions: Pastors must know when to expand their programs and facilities by debt financing (bank loans or other financing), or by using cash and/or consolidating assets and focusing internally for growth.

Networking: Today's urban pastor must have access to political leaders and key community leaders in order to successfully tap into all the resources available to fund the programs needed to meet the vast needs people have— especially in an urban context.

Business/Administration: Most pastors are good preachers, but I have noticed that many of the most successful churches are those run by leaders with a business background. This is why I tell all those training for the ministry to get at least an associates degree in business finance.

Just having anointed services on Sunday cannot build a successful church. You must have continual vision casting, strategic planning with 3-5 year goals, implementation and administration of the vision, leadership development, discipleship training, team building, selecting and funding the proper gift mix for your staff, and much more.

2. Learning how to relate the gospel to your audience

Many preachers are answering questions their audience is not asking. Pastors need to have the skill and the information to gauge the demographic make-up of their community, and know how to connect to their communities. Connection is based on the age, ethnicity, economic, and religious context of a community.

Pastors need to constantly monitor the sociological trends in their communities so they can raise up the leadership necessary to relate to the people who will be the dominant groups in their communities. For example, because of gentrification, a community like Harlem may be mostly Caucasian in coming years. African-American pastors in this community need to know how to adjust their outreach to their community. Or, consider opening up satellite churches or ministries to reach those presently in their church who may move to the suburbs. Thus, pastors need to skillfully exegete their communities, not just the Scriptures.

3. Leadership development

How does the church effectively transform new believers from babes into responsible, mature members? How does the church effectively mentor potential leaders who have 10-hour workdays and 2-3 hour daily commutes to and from work? Usually those with the potential to lead already have responsible positions at their jobs. Thus, they are already spent and weary before they come to church and minister.

Pastors must answer the question: Are we going to be a program-based church, or are we going to depend on empowering lay leadership for shepherding (the cell church model)?

4. Board development issues

Pastors have to answer the questions: What is the biblical model of local church government? What model of church government will we follow? Also, who should the pastor select to be on the church's board of trustees? This changes based on the maturity of your leadership, type of church government, the age of your church, the history of your church, and if the pastor is the founder or entering into an already-developed board.

5. The lack of a safe place

Most pastors lack true accountability. Organizational accountability in most denominations does not ensure true accountability based on vulnerable, transparent relationships. Many will not go to those over them or peers within their own denominations for fear they will be stigmatized and will not be able to move up in the organization.

All pastors need other pastors over them as mentors and peer relationships with others they can trust in transparent relationships for self-renewal. Legendary English spiritual leader John Wesley once said, "The Bible knows nothing of solitary religion. Christianity is a religion of fellowship."

Most pastors feel isolated and alone, even in the midst of their congregation. Many pastors are comfortable in the pulpit because they hide behind their anointing and their ministry gifting but are socially dysfunctional, never allowing anyone to really know them or relate to them to establish a real emotional connection. Even when they are with other pastors, the bulk of their conversations are about ministry and not about personal issues like marriage, the state of their inner lives, or the challenges of raising children.

6. Tension between spiritual leader role and organizational leader role

Many pastors do not know how to distinguish their roles as pastor/shepherd from leader of the organization in which they have to hire and fire, based on maintaining a spirit of excellence in business. There is great stress in knowing when and how to fire staff who may be faithful members in the church the pastor is shepherding. They need skill (training) as to both the business and spiritual aspects of the church.

Another problem is that many pastors do not know how to balance their time between administration and spiritual preparation, and are spending 40 hours per week in administration. Acts 6:4 teaches administration is primarily the work of deacons, yet a large percentage of pastors are neglecting their time in studying Scripture and praying in the presence of God. This results in pastors burning out because the needs of the people are pulling on their grace gifting to come forth, but they are not able to give it because their spiritual tank is empty.

7. Compassion fatigue

Many pastors are so used to just giving and giving that they do not know how and when to receive. Sometimes I would come to places where I was working so hard for so long that I actually felt guilty when I had some time off for rest; I literally did not know how to rest. On many vacations, I needed at least three days before my mind and emotions caught up to my body so that I was able to mentally adjust to taking time off!

God has placed sacred rhythms in our lives so that there would be regular times of refreshing and renewal. God calls the Sabbath "a sign between us and Him." What is the sign? That He is God and that our church or work will not fall apart when we take time off because He is the one building the church (Matthew 16:18-19)!

Life is not a marathon but a series of 100-meter dashes. We need to continually take time to rest and regroup before we go out to run the race again. Because I am filled with so much vision, I often hate the fact that my body gets tired and needs 6-8 hours of sleep per night. But then I realize that God did this on purpose—not to rest my body but primarily to rest my mind and emotions so that I can start each morning with a fresh perspective.

Most pastors can trace burnout to not regularly replenishing their souls with rest, prayer, reading, fellowship, exercise, and caring for their emotional lives. We can renew ourselves by doing things that we enjoy; it does not always have to be prayer, study, or a spiritual or religious discipline. It can be viewing art, playing a sport, spending time with one's spouse, having a social life, or simply having a hobby that you enjoy.

8. Many pastors do not know how to build a dream team, and have people operating outside of their gift mix

Accurately placing people based on their giftings is one of the most important things in terms of releasing a pastor from some of their responsibilities in the ministry. God has called our churches to function as apostolic centers, wherein all the ministry gifts of Ephesians 4:11 can function so the work of the ministry or the oversight of the church is not dependent on any one person.

Every pastor should have the Antioch church as their model—one where the church is shepherded by a diverse multiplicity of ministers (Acts 13:1). This can prevent the church overseer from reaching ministerial burnout because they will have the ability to balance their time between work, family, private renewal, and relaxation.

Every dream team is made up of at least four kinds of leaders:
1. *Visionary or directional leader*: The one who motivates the church and casts a macro vision.
2. *Strategic leader*: The person who lays out the strategic plan on how to implement the vision.
3. *The team builder*: The "people person" who spends time among the sheep and builds the morale of the office staff or ministry team.
4. *The operational leader*: The one who loves to create systems and leaves paper trails for proper protocol to operate in the church.

9. The unique contribution of each kind of leader:

Macro leaders, like directional leaders, become impatient when bogged down dealing with high-maintenance "problem people." This is a job for the pastors and/or team builders. Macro leaders are wired to spend their time with those who contribute to the big picture and bring them the biggest return from their very busy schedule.

Strategic leaders are perfectionists who have a hard time making deadlines and pulling the trigger on important decisions.

The team builders who are given a heavy administration workload will get frustrated. Unlike the operational leaders, they hate paperwork!

Asking operational leaders, strategic leaders, and team builders to cast vision will only hinder the church and frustrate these three leaders. This is a job only the directional leader can do correctly.

One time a senior pastor I was overseeing asked me to mediate a problem between him and one of his staff pastors. I had to tell him after we spoke for half an hour that this staff person was misplaced. The senior pastor was trying to get this (team building) leader to be an administrator, and the result was both pastors were frustrated and almost parted ways.

(For more on this concept, read *A Fish Out of Water: 9 Strategies Effective Leaders Use to Help You Get Back into the Flow* by George Barna.)

10. Competition among churches (or pastors)

Unfortunately, many leaders are driven by self and not led by the Spirit. They are especially driven by their need to feel significant based on the growth and success of other churches in their community or region. This is a serious issue among some pastors and causes much self-induced stress and feelings of inadequacy, depression, and insecurity.

When a leader endeavors to grow a church numerically without commensurate church health, it is a sure sign that the leader is driven more by ego and/or insecurity than the pure desire of obeying their God-given assignment. Because of this competitive spirit, some pastors secretly celebrate when a fellow pastor is struggling; they also secretly become discouraged when a church in their community prospers and grows more than theirs. This is a sure sign of unhealthy competition.

One reason for this is because pastors become confused when a church in their community is blessed and their church does not grow as fast. This causes them to wonder what they are doing wrong and what the other pastor is doing right. Thus, they are driven by insecurity. In 2 Corinthians 12:2, Paul teaches leaders not to compare themselves with others.

When pastors understand that the Kingdom of God is greater than their local church, then competitive feelings will begin to dissipate.

11. Lack of personal vision/life plan

Many leaders are personally lost even when they have a great vision for their church. They are not sure who they are, what their assignment is, or how to lead based on their strengths. Thus, it is possible to attempt to lead a congregation and cast a vision without even being sure of your specific assignment from the Lord! There are also people who pastor a church only because they do not know of any other way to make a living; they are really evangelists, teachers, prophets, or marketplace leaders, trying to function in the mold of a pastor although they do not have a nurturing bone in their body!

12. Many leaders don't know how to lead

Some leaders depend on positional leadership based on their title, rather than functional leadership. I was shocked years ago when I realized that not all pastors are leaders. Someone with little or no mantle of leadership trying to lead a congregation will eventually lead to people going in their own direction, looking for the real leader in their midst.

I agree with George Barna (as stated in his book, *A Fish Out of Water*) when he says that there are habitual leaders (born leaders) who are so gifted that leadership comes naturally to them; they simply intuit leadership.

I also agree with bestselling author and leadership expert John Maxwell, who says we can grow as leaders by asking people to mentor us and by taking the time to study about leadership. God has called each leader to know and articulate their own mission statement.

Solutions

1. Pastors need to find peer communities with compatible vision where they will find a safe haven to receive from and aid them in fulfilling their vision. Denominational presbytery meetings do not necessarily meet this need.
2. Pastors need one or more other pastors who will coach them, hold them accountable, and speak to the needs of their emotional and inner lives.

3. Pastors need to erect boundaries and firewalls around themselves and their families so that their personal lives and families will have time to replenish and be renewed.
4. Pastors need to take care of their physical bodies with regular exercise, solitude and silence, rest, and proper diet.
5. Pastors need to take regular times of rest and/or sabbaticals: (1) 1 year for every 7 years in ministry. I realize this may not be possible for bi-vocational pastors or those in small, rural congregations, but it is possible to take creative steps by using guest ministers and deacons or elders to give the pastor an extended break.(2) 1 day for every 7 days. (3) 3 days away for prayer and reflection every 3 months.
6. Pastors need to pay attention to their emotional needs, not just their spiritual lives.
7. Pastors need to take care of their intellectual lives. Some pastors should go back to school. The majority of pastors in many regions have less than a bachelor's degree; thus, most lack serious, well-ordered learning. Pastors should prioritize regular times for study to develop their intellect and regular times for devotional reading. Just reading to preach is work and will wear you out and not necessarily draw you closer to God.
8. Pastors need to bring their spouses along in all facets of self-renewal and ministry so that there is unity and compatibility of vision in their marriages.

Now, I spent this chapter reviewing a multiplicity of challenges pastors face, and why some give up. But at the same time, leaders should recognize that failure is not a reason to throw up their arms and quit. In chapter 6, I will review how failure can be the gateway to success.

Recommended Resources

Sacred Rhythms: Arranging Our Lives for Spiritual Transformation, by Ruth Haley Barton

Invitation to Solitude and Silence: Experiencing God's Transforming Presence, by Ruth Haley Barton

The Emotionally Healthy Church, by Peter Scazzero

A Fish Out of Water: 9 Strategies Effective Leaders Use to Help You Get Back into the Flow, by George Barna

CHAPTER 6

HOW FAILURE CAN EMPOWER SUCCESS

Every year we should reflect on the successes and failures of the past twelve months, using both as a trajectory toward a more productive experience in the future.

By "success" I am referring to fruit borne to the glory of God that expanded Kingdom influence. By "failure" I mean anything we initiated or participated in that did not bear any noticeable fruit. Failure can also be defined as when a paradigm, strategy of life, or ministry is no longer producing the results we set out to obtain.

During my ministry I have been through many stages and cycles of ministry, and have experienced both success and failure. I have learned the hard way to embrace failure as part of the normal process of learning. The older I get, the more experience I have, and hopefully the fewer intense lessons of failure I need to experience in my life journey.

Since Christ is the redeemer of all failure and sin, Christianity is replete with success stories with a perspective that utilizes failure—and even evil—for good. Joseph told his brothers in Genesis 50 that what they meant for evil, God meant for good. The Apostle James tells us that we should count it pure joy when we fall into diverse tests, because the outworking of these tests develops our character (James 1:3-4). Jesus's suffering resulted in His glorious resurrection.

Thus, the Bible has a theology of success that can come out of any failure we experience—if we respond to God in faith and humility. Romans 8:28 says that all things work together for good for those who love God. One of the greatest discoveries I have made is that, as a Christ-follower, I can't lose. Even when I fail, I can seize failure as an opportunity for further growth so I can go to another level of success. Every situation and circumstance, no matter how difficult, can be redeemed for good!

Following are some reasons failure can empower success:

1. Failure causes us to rethink our current paradigm of ministry

If scientists and innovators in technology treated failure the way leaders in ministry do, then scientific and technological progress would be stifled! Those in fields of research understand that, for every failed experiment, they are closer to proving or disproving their hypotheses. Failure in ministry or business has the power to get us to recalibrate how we operate and make us more efficient. Even the corrections in the market economy during the past several years are part of a normal cycle of allowing what really works to come to the forefront, and correct some of the systemic ills regarding our cultural business habits.

2. Failure can bring greater humility

God has used ministry and relational failure to bring me closer to Him and to rely on Him more for my well-being, identity, and success. As a younger leader, I could only reach a certain point of humility on my own, based on Bible reading and private devotion. God had to use the fiery trials of life experience that come over time to work a deeper level of humility in my soul.

3. Failure can bring more compassion towards others

Struggles with my own children have given me more compassion with Christian parents who have their own family challenges. I have found that I have far more authority to speak and minister to people in the areas I have been the most challenged in, especially because my heart resonates with people who are going through the same battles I have experienced.

4. Failure can cause us to seek God more earnestly

The longer I am in church ministry the more I realize that I will never get the results I seek in our local church, network, or public life without seeking God earnestly. I have found that when I initiate ministry—based on my own natural gifts and abilities to lead and strategize—then it is up to me to keep it going in my own strength. God is not obligated to empower that which He never willed to exist! The older I get the more I try never to get involved in anything unless it not only fits my purpose and mission, but also comes out of a strong witness of God's leading in the Holy Spirit during prayer and contemplation.

5. Failure can make us more interdependent with other key leaders

As a young leader, I had hoped God was going to use me to bring great revival to New York City. But several years into our young ministry, I went to hell and back (figuratively) and experienced much suffering, due to failures in key relationships and ministry. After several years of intense trauma, I came out of those trials with an understanding of how much I needed other leaders. This resulted in an intense desire to network key leaders and churches from around the city, which gave birth to "All City Prayer" initiatives starting in 1991, in which more than 1,000 people and more than 50 churches and leaders would come together for a day of fasting and prayer for our city. That was followed by many other citywide initiatives too numerous to mention. (Read my book, *Kingdom Awakening*, for more on these initiatives.) All of this was precipitated by my experiencing failure in multiple areas related to family and ministry.

6. Failure can make us more self-aware

One of the greatest lessons from failure is that it made me more aware of who I am and what makes me tick; it helps me realize when I am being driven by fleshly, personal ambition or when I am being led by the Lord. Every time I experience failure I use it as an opportunity to self-reflect and learn how and why I did what I did.

7. Failure can become an empowering message of wisdom for other younger leaders

I spend a lot of time mentoring younger leaders. One of the most fruitful times I have in those sessions is when I am sharing with them areas of my failures and the reasons that led to them. Without these compelling stories, I would not be equipped with the wisdom I need to encourage and exhort these younger, less experienced leaders.

8. Failure can force us to kick in our faith for God's miraculous power

Zechariah 4:7 is more real to me today than ever. Truly I have found that, when all is said and done, it is not by my power or might things happen. It takes God's Spirit to accomplish His will and purposes in the earth. Failure has taught me the vast limitations of depending on my natural gifts and abilities to minister in His Kingdom. When I hit a leadership wall and have no solutions, God reminds me that it is going to take faith in His ability to intervene and perform a miracle to accomplish His will!

9. Failure can force us to change our priorities in life

One of the greatest lessons I have learned in leadership is realizing that knowing *what not to do* is just as important as knowing *what to do*. I get numerous opportunities and invitations to minister locally, nationally, and internationally. If I took every good opportunity that comes my way (that fits my mission and purpose in life) I would lose my center of gravity and become less effective in my key relationships in family and ministry. I have learned that it is a huge mistake to equate mere activity with significance. Failure has helped shape my core priorities in life that are centered in seeking God, personal study, family relationships, and mentoring key and emerging leaders. Everything else has to take a back seat!

10. Failure can ground us more in reality and pragmatism

Often, when we go from one successful endeavor to another, we lose our sense of reality and begin to take things for granted (like doing due diligence before making important decisions and commitments to others). Failure shakes us up and brings us more to the ground level of how the world really operates. It can also be the impetus of acquiring more discernment.

11. Failure can cause us to construct better models for others to follow

Ultimately, every failure should become a building block for us to construct a better model of how we live and lead. It can force us to pause in this hectic world and grapple for balance and proper rhythm. It enables us to see what really works as opposed to what is an unworkable concept.

When new ministries or churches start and experience immediate success and church growth, it pains me to see the senior pastor becoming a mentor or coach before they know if their ministry model is sustainable over the long haul! For example, there are some pastors whose churches have experienced enormous growth and are writing books and giving advice to a new generation of leaders. Yet, they lead local churches that are less than 10 years old. This is too early to tell if their model can withstand the test of time in regard to ministry burnout, leadership turnover, and multi-generational success in developing healthy families who will keep their children and perpetuate the faith. I don't believe we can trust models and philosophies of ministry until they have experienced the fiery trials of failure and come out on the other side!

THE BIBLICAL VIEW OF FAILURE

Failure is an important topic because so many of us are driven to succeed more by a fear of failure than by the call of God on our life. This is partly because in this nation we have a "black and white" view of success and failure that deems failure unacceptable. The following are additional points we need to understand regarding the biblical view of failure.

1. Failure is something we are all born into

Psalm 51:5 teaches us that "in sin did my mother conceive me," Romans 3:23 teaches that all of us have sinned and fallen short of the glory of God. In light of these passages, we understand every human being, from Cain and Abel to ourselves today, has started from a foundation of falling short of God's perfection, standards, and expectations. Some people try to get around this by rationalizing it away, justifying sin, or becoming despondent and living a life of guilt and depression without hope.

God has given us another way out. He uses our failures to make us aware of the sin in our system so we would seek out a Savior. The law becomes our schoolmaster to lead us to Christ because of how utterly sinful we are (Galatians 3:24 and Romans 7:13).

2. Failure is meant to teach us the truth

As I mentioned earlier, if scientists viewed failure the way most do in ministry, we could well still be living in the Dark Ages! Instead of becoming discouraged and quitting when their hypotheses fail, they look at failure as part of the continuum of finding the truth. When we fail, in most cases we can look at it the same way: as a learning experience that enables us to get closer to knowing what to do in the future when faced with similar situations. The trick is, we need to learn how to "fail forward."

This idea is strongly opposed to the way our present culture operates. Men love sports so much because there are always clear winners and losers. I will never forget the sports headline on one of the major New York newspapers in recent years after the Mets blew a seven-game lead late in the season several summers ago. (Not too long after that, they then fell out of contention on the final day of the season!) The headline included, "Choked" or something with that word in it. But unfortunately this all-or-nothing approach often wreaks havoc with our psyches, from undue stress based on the expectation to always be a clear winner in everything we do.

I believe having high standards is necessary to gauge excellence in sports, grading students, and so on. But I also believe that in the complexities of life we are meant to fail at times, so we can have epiphanies and learn the greater lessons we would have never learned had we been "successful" in our initial course of action.

3. God has to orchestrate success or failure

The Scriptures teach that God works all things for good if we love Him (Romans 8:28). This means God maneuvers things because we do not always get it right the first time. I am convinced that sometimes, in order for us to really learn certain things, we need to initially fail as part of the process of God ingraining truth into our souls. Also, if we were successful with everything we did, then we would get the glory instead of God. The fact that God has to step in and work all things out for good in response to our sincere love for Him demonstrates that, ultimately, all success is really attributed to God based on His divine intervention, whether overt or subtle.

Scripture is replete with examples of leaders who, at first, lived lives as failures so that God could have a chance to turn them around:

- Adam had to be covered after he fell (Genesis 3)
- Jacob was a deceiver whom God had to wrestle with and change before he would become a man of God (Genesis 27-32)
- Moses had to flee Egypt as a murderer and live in the desert for 40 years before God was able to teach him enough to use him (Exodus 1-3)
- Samson failed as a son, husband, and believer before he was able to defeat the Philistines with his last act (Judges 15-16)
- David lost everything, including his wife, best friend, and possessions before he was anointed as king (I and II Samuel)
- Peter denied Jesus three times right before he became the leader of the early church and won three thousand people to Christ on the Day of Pentecost (Matthew 26-27; Acts 1-2)
- Saul was a murderer and persecutor of Christians before he became the great Apostle Paul (Acts 8-28)

As you can see, failure is part of the redemptive method of teaching God uses to mature us into His people with purposeful assignments to enlarge kingdom influence. As much as we hate it, and in spite of the fact God has called us to avoid failing intentionally (If we fail intentionally in life, we will not learn because we are not properly stewarding the gifts and grace God has given us to serve Him and humanity.), we will all experience failure—some on greater levels than others.

Hebrews 12:5-11 teaches us that whom the Lord loves He rebukes and chastens. I am thankful that, in spite of my weaknesses and failures, I have a mighty God and a community of covenant people God uses in my life who can teach me when I am wrong, pick me up when I fall, and push me forward when I fail.

A final word about failure: we can get our sights out of whack when we consider it the ultimate humiliation. In the same way, we can swing to the other extreme and think the biggest, greatest, flashiest, or dazzling thing is a sign of success and God's blessings. In the next chapter, I will pose the question of whether the Apostle Paul would have been considered a success.

CHAPTER 7

WOULD THE APOSTLE PAUL BE CONSIDERED A SUCCESS TODAY?

MANY, IF NOT MOST, scholars consider the Apostle Paul the most important leader in the history of the church—with the exception of the Lord Jesus Christ. Paul's influence cannot be overstated in spite of the fact he never had oversight of a megachurch (having started small house churches in about 30 cities); he wasn't very prosperous (often speaking about being hungry, thirsty, and naked, as in 1 Corinthians 4:11); he wasn't a celebrity leader (frequently being met by mobs of angry people wanting to kill him, as in Acts 9:23 and 14:19); he was not very well-known during his lifetime outside the cities and regions where he planted churches (his fame spreading beyond these regions after through his letters to the churches); and he was diminutive, not necessarily good looking, and may not have been a great orator (2 Corinthians 10:10).

This says a lot about how today's standards for measuring success stack up against the values God laid out in Scripture. I have asked myself the question: If Paul were alive today, based on what is mentioned above, would he ever have been a celebrity preacher or been featured on the front pages of newspapers and Christian magazines?

Too often the American Dream has tainted our standards for success! Because of this, some younger pastors are more swayed by the standards of the secular world than biblical standards regarding priorities, focus, ambitions, and goals. As I read the New Testament, I see that there were several key reasons why Paul has had so much historical influence and impact:

1. He developed spiritual sons and daughters

He called Timothy his son and developed him into apostolic ministry, which evidently was his pattern for ministry. When he wrote to the Corinthian church, he emphasized that he was their father in the gospel, not just a teacher (1 Corinthians 4:15).

Unfortunately, much of the focus today in the church is on drawing crowds and having a great worship experience. Few lead pastors are nurturing sons and daughters in the faith through personal mentoring because it is not as "sexy" and public as other aspects of the ministry.

2. He poured into key leaders who could reproduce others

Paul showed that the key to establishing strong churches was to take aside faithful, capable people with the gift of teaching, disciple them, and release them to minister to the congregation (2 Timothy 2:2). This also goes along with the Jethro Principle that Moses followed in Exodus 18:15-23, in which the primary leader focuses on developing those with the potential to lead others, so masses of people can be cared for without leadership burnout. Paul also understood how

God places leaders in the body of Christ so the foundation of the church is solid (1 Corinthians 12:28-31).

3. He established solid churches in key cities

Paul had a vision for urban ministry and planted churches in the main cities of the Roman Empire. For example, in the New Testament we see Paul concentrated much of his ministry in Philippi, Colossae, Thessalonica, Corinth, Ephesus, Antioch, Jerusalem, Laconia, Derbe, and other cities. He went where the most people lived so the gospel could have a transcultural, trans-regional, and multi-generational impact!

4. He developed a complex apostolic network that has lasted for 2,000 years

Every house church Paul established eventually led to establishing other house churches in the same city, which eventually led to a network of house churches in each city. Each networked city church then became an apostolic hub that networked with all the other city church networks, all held together by authoritative apostolic letters and sent-out itinerant leaders. Thus, Paul became a master at building complex apostolic networks that were able to communicate the gospel to the polytheistic, multilingual, and multiethnic cultures of his day.

5. He was able to identify the main issues and write about them under the inspiration of the Holy Spirit

Paul was so connected relationally with each house church through his complex apostolic system of networking that he was able to have his ear to the ground and address problems before they got out of hand and a church was destroyed. (Read the letters to the Galatians, Thessalonians, and Philippians.) Not only that, but the letters he wrote were so saturated with prayer and the inspiration, wisdom, and doctrine of the Holy Spirit that God has used them to make up a large portion of our New Testament, which has instructed billions of believers for more than 2,000 years!

6. He was courageous and faithful under persecution

Paul was so devoted to Christ and His church that he lived as a dead man on furlough. It didn't matter if he was stoned to death; he went right back to the same city after he was raised back to life to continue to preach the gospel (Acts 14:19-20)! He wrote in Philippians that he wanted to magnify Christ in his body, whether by life or by death (Phil. 1:20-21).

7. He was passionate about Jesus Christ and kept first things first

The secret of Paul's success was his ability to forget his past success and continue to keep his head and his heart on the greatest prize in the universe: the Lord Jesus Christ. Paul said that he counted all things as dung in order that he may win Christ and that it was not he who lived, but Christ who lived through him (Philippians 3:1-15 and Galatians 2:20). Today too many leaders forget that their main obligation is not to the people they minister to, but to love and seek the Lord, who called them to minister!

8. He learned how to be strong in his weaknesses

While most leaders today brag about their ministry successes, Paul learned to glory in his weaknesses so the power of Christ could rest on him (2 Corinthians 12:1-7). He understood that, because of human pride, God has to allow adverse circumstances in our lives to buffet us, so we too will learn to trust in God who raises the dead (2 Corinthians 1:9). (I don't know of one high-level leader in the world who doesn't live with incredible challenges–either in their personal life or ministry!)

Paul was so used to ministering in his weakness and with physical discomfort that he was able to worship the Lord in prison, even after being beaten and chained (Acts 16), which released an incredible move of God that resulted in a revival in Europe. Paul knew that every adverse situation in his life would be turned around for the good of the gospel so that, no matter what Satan threw at him, Christ would always be glorified in the end (Philippians 1:12-14)!

9. He had an incredible love for the church and His kingdom

Paul was constantly concerned with the state of the churches he founded. He was constantly longing to be with those he led to Christ (Philippians 1:8) and follow them up (Acts 15:36). Too often we have a goal of winning souls without a plan for nurturing, training, and assimilating these souls into the church. Jesus made it very clear that if we love Him we would feed His sheep (John 21:15-17).

10. He finished well

Unfortunately, many of the leaders who walked with Paul responded like the Twelve Apostles of Jesus when He was arrested: they forsook him! After his arrest, Paul wrote to Timothy that no one stood with him except Luke (2 Timothy 4:9-11).

Many have told me that a high percentage of successful leaders do not finish well. Paul did. This is what he wrote to Timothy in his final letter preceding his imminent death: "I am already being poured out as a drink offering (torture?) and the time of my departure is at hand. I have fought the good fight, I have finished the race, I have kept the faith. Henceforth there is laid up for me the crown of righteousness, which the Lord, the righteous judge, will award to me on that day, and not only to me but also to all who have loved His appearing" (2 Timothy 4:6-8).

In light of the life of Paul, I believe that we, as the body of Christ, need to redefine our goals and measures of success so we can also finish the race with joy and lay our crowns at the feet of Jesus on the last day.

Considering the lessons we can glean from Paul's example, we need to consider whose kingdom we are building: ours or God's. In chapter 8, I will review some sure signs that you are constructing your own empire instead of the Kingdom that will last.

CHAPTER 8

BUILDING EMPIRES BUT NOT GOD'S KINGDOM

Ever since the divide of the Western and Eastern branches of Christianity in the 11th century, two of the greatest fears of once-united Christendom have been realized: fragmentation and division. Even in the 16th century, when Martin Luther's protest against the Roman Catholic Church's abuses sparked the Protestant Reformation, leaders hoped there would be only a few major expressions of the body of Christ. Never in their wildest dreams did the reformers envision all the denominations and various branches and networks of Christianity that have evolved since then. The end results have provided an opportunity for a spirit of lawlessness, independence, and empire-building among some insecure (albeit gifted) leaders.

It is not my purpose to judge whether all these expressions are of God or not. However, the following list will reveal some signs when the motivation to build a church, ministry, or network is akin to the human race's attempt to build its own empire, epitomized by the Tower of Babel—which God judged and scattered across the whole earth (Genesis 11:1-18).

In 1 Kings 11:11 and 12:16, God divided the kingdom of Israel because of religious apostasy, which is the same reason the Roman Catholic Church was corrected and fragmented (too much concentration of power in the hands of humans, who deviated from the true way of Jesus and the apostles). God will judge His church and hold back revival from certain churches, ministries, and regions when their key spiritual leaders are attempting to build themselves empires instead of God's Kingdom. Such leaders may talk the talk, but their actions often speak louder than their so-called "Kingdom-first" words.

The following are 17 signs you are an empire builder instead of a Kingdom builder:

1. You rejoice when other key leaders in your region are struggling

Although all leaders with their mouths say they are sad when another church, pastor, or leader in their area is struggling, I have observed that some leaders seem to privately gloat or compare themselves with other failing leaders in their area. Whether the failing church or leader is right or wrong, it never pleases God when we internally rejoice or gloat when the body of Christ is not advancing in our region.

2. You are territorial and only work with those under your "covering"

Some leaders and denominations I know will only do outreaches with churches and leaders with whom they have a ministerial and financial allegiance. If we are going to reach our communities, we have to be willing to cross denominations and networks and work with the leaders who are sincerely committed to advancing the Kingdom.

3. You only support events that can give you a platform

I have seen leaders actually pull out of a citywide or community event because their names were not advertised on the program, or because someone they are rivals with was part of the program. This shows that their concern was not advancing the Kingdom, but advancing their own name and empire-building goals.

4. You tend to exaggerate your own importance and influence with outsiders

Empire builders treat their ministries like a sporting event. They are constantly throwing around numbers and statistics while comparing their numbers to the numbers of other ministers. They say things like, "We are growing in record numbers," "This was the most significant event in our city," or, "We have the largest network in our city." Or, worse yet, they claim something like, "Our ministry is the reason why the crime rate went down in our community (or region)." Furthermore, they tend to exaggerate their influence, importance, and results in their region or community.

In contrast, Kingdom builders brag about what God is doing through His church in His city. They also attempt to applaud the success of others whose feet they wash, instead of propping themselves up for photo shoots and publicity. I have observed that several so-called revivals in our country in recent years have been more or less attributable to good advertising and marketing, rather than a real move of God.

5. You are jealous of successful key leaders in your region

I know I am with an empire builder when I am with a person who is always attempting to dig up dirt on other leaders, criticizing key leaders in their community, or giving "faint praise" when asked about other key leaders in their region.

6. You speak about Kingdom unity as a smokescreen to hide your own selfish agenda

Some of the most self-centered empire builders I have known in the past four decades have spoken the most in public about the need for unity in the body of Christ. They use this kind of talk to get "sheep pastors and ministers" to forsake their own agendas and follow them to aid them in building their empires! They know the entire lingo and have the biblical passages down, but unfortunately their actions do not correspond with their words and preaching.

7. Your name and picture must be highlighted in every event you participate in

I have heard leaders speak about God raising up a movement of "nameless" and "faceless" people. Yet, in all their conferences, literature, and advertising, their picture and name are highlighted more than anyone or anything else in the program. I attended one conference in which there was a life-size picture of the leader in the lobby, with the event and program advertised in small print under his picture!

8. You try to steal the loyalties of people connected to other ministries

One of the key signs that someone is an empire builder is when they go after key leaders in other leaders' churches or networks. I myself have had leaders in our Christ Covenant Coalition approached by another leader in our city, asking them to join his network as a representative, even though these leaders have been part of my leadership for over 10 years. When leaders do this, they make themselves look bad—both to the loyal leaders they approach and to the other key leaders in the city who eventually find out about the modus operandi of this empire builder.

9. You love those who follow you and disregard all others

Empire builders have an "either you are with me or against me" mentality and approach to life. Empire builders will not be friends with a person if they are also connected to the ministry of a rival. One of my regional leaders was told several years ago that he was no longer welcome to preach in a particular church because he was keeping the company of a certain other leader (me). Since empire builders are untrustworthy and use their pseudo friendships as a platform to perpetuate their own empires, they project that same spirit and mentality on other leaders in their region. Thus, they cut off people loyal to other networks and ministries because they suspect others are as untrustworthy as they are!

10. You have a "top down" leadership approach, and thus struggle to attract strong, successful leaders

Empire builders surround themselves with "yes men" and discourage strong, resourceful leaders from working or partnering with them because it does not fit their "top down" leadership style. Unlike mature leaders who take a "bottom up" approach, in which they try to lead through consensus with participation of various levels of people taking responsibility in ministry (so that all have ownership in the process), empire builders surround themselves with leaders of ministries they deem less significant. They want leaders who will follow their dictates without meaningful, strategic dialogue.

11. You are driven by self, not led by the Spirit

Your intense need for affirmation because of your insecurities drives your need for success, not the glory of God and the work of advancing the Kingdom. Thus, there is rarely inner peace or rest because you are striving, constantly trying to create a platform and expand your ministry on your own efforts, instead of being led by the Lord and letting Him bring you opportunities and open doors.

12. You are an opportunist when other ministries are struggling

Empire builders make believe they are concerned when other churches or ministries are struggling, but they attempt to maneuver themselves so they can capitalize on the struggles of other ministries and either seize their property or, more likely, their choicest leaders and key people.

13. Your main goal in life is to build some kind of monument to your success

Empire builders are obsessed with building bigger and better buildings and acquiring more and more property—even if they have to take on huge debt. The lower their self-esteem, the bigger they have to build to compensate for their internal lack. Unfortunately, they are often risking the future of their ministry with all this spending. They rarely, if ever, think about how their successor is going to fill all these buildings and pay off the mortgage. Remember, there is never any real success without a successor!

14. When possible, you will sabotage the influence and ministry of other leaders you deem a threat to your influence

Recently, I reunited with a key leader in another country after almost 12 years of disconnect. I tried numerous times to stay connected, but could never understand why there seemed to be some kind of obstruction in our relationship. After speaking for three hours, it finally dawned on us that another leader who was jealous of my influence in this country sabotaged our relationship because he wanted to supplant me as the spiritual covering for this key leader. I have also witnessed first-hand one leader use innuendo and lies about another key leader behind their back, in an attempt to stop their influence from spreading to other regions. In instances like these, we need to speak up and defend the honor of those not present in the room.

15. You tend to copy those you are jealous of in your region

It is said that when someone copies your ideas, it is the highest form of flattery. Empire builders will attempt to replicate and outdo many of the things other key leaders in their region are doing. They may call it something different, but in the end it is essentially the same model, but with the attitude of making it bigger and better than anything else in their region. It is like Dunkin' (Donuts) or McDonald's trying to reinvent themselves to keep up with Starbucks. It is born out of personal competition and not a pure love for Christ and His Kingdom.

16. You are a narcissist in relating to your desires in life

Ultimately, empire builders are lovers of themselves. Thus, they will sacrifice the dreams and lives of others so their own dreams can be fulfilled. They will throw everyone and anyone under the bus to advance their goals or save their own skin! Their incredible commitment to the ministry is really only a commitment to advance their own ideals and dreams, which is narcissistic in nature. This is unlike the model of Christ, who laid down His own life for the sheep. Ezekiel 34 speaks about the judgment God will bring on shepherds who use and abuse the sheep for their own pleasure.

17. You tell people that your church or network is the main key in your city for true revival and transformation

When giving reports about your ministry, you exaggerate the results of your work and utilize self-serving testimonies that back up your claim of spiritual dominance in your region. Many pastors I know have told me of prophecies that have come forth, alluding to the fact that it is their church that is going to start a revival for the nation or their community, or that revival is going to start in their region and go to the world because their region is the gate to the rest of the country. I am tired of hearing these prophecies and so-called words from the Lord.

Unfortunately, some prophets are motivated to give these flattering words so they can get invited back to preach; they know that most inexperienced leaders fall prey to prophetic flattery. That being said, empire builders use these words, visions, and experiences to back up their claims that their particular church or ministry is "the church" in their region God is going to use so they can garner the loyalties of unsuspecting and naive sheep, and even pastors.

In my experience, most churches with that attitude are judged by God and actually begin to decline until the leaders repent of pride. Although it is possible that revival can come through one church to the whole world (Think the Azusa Street Revival in 1906.), it is the exception to the rule. Community, city, and national transformations usually take place when God visits a region or nation, and multitudes of churches receive "times of refreshing" simultaneously. This results in the formation of informal apostolic networks, which partner together to continue to perpetuate the advance of the Kingdom of God.

It is sad when God's people engage in personal empire building and career advancement over ministry and service to His children. Such fleshly habits fuel the toxic leadership we see often in the modern church.

Before I move on to discuss leadership problems in Part II, though, I want to offer a word of warning to pastors about the "problem children" they will have to learn to deal with in ministry. I call them the kinds of people nobody can help.

CHAPTER 9

THE KINDS OF PEOPLE NOBODY CAN HELP

I HAVE LEARNED THE hard way that I cannot help every person who attends our church or who comes to me for input. The following are ten kinds of people I have identified who are so entrenched in certain habit patterns that I cannot help them advance to the next level unless they make the necessary shift in their attitude or behavior:

1. Those who do not take responsibility for themselves

The first step towards self-improvement is to remove all excuses for mediocrity or failure. Those who continually blame other people for their failures will never go to the next level. Leaders can complain about things like their spouses, the income level of their congregations, or the lack of staff, but I have learned that within every challenge is the seed of opportunity for success which requires the creativity of problem solving.

2. Those who do not have a heart to seek God

The Bible teaches that "the fear of the Lord is the beginning of wisdom" (Proverbs 9:10, ESV). Those who do not respect God enough to seek Him and study His Word so they can make wise decisions in life are violating Scripture (Joshua 1:8-9) and cannot be helped either by myself or any other leader or minister. Those who do not obey what God requires for success have decided to try to be successful in life without God's blessings!

3. Those who create distance so they are not accountable

There are certain people I have met in our church who cut relationships off before a person can get close to them. Many go from one church to the next because they fear becoming too close to a leader who will hold them accountable. Often some will attempt to attend a megachurch where they will be able to hear the Word of God in the context of a large crowd, so that no one will really know who they are. Whether it is fear or rebellion, those who live like this have put a low ceiling on their lives and will not grow past the infant stage concerning their potential in life.

4. Those who insist on having a negative outlook on life

There are some people who refuse to exercise faith in God or think positively as the Word of God commands in Philippians 4:8. This is because some have a propensity to expect the worst in life so they are never disappointed by anyone or anything! This is a weird way some folks attempt to shield their emotions from the pain of disappointment. Jesus often told people that they would receive according to how they believed (Matthew 8:13). Proverbs 23:7 says that as a person thinks in their heart, so they will be. I cannot empower a person who refuses to think God's thoughts about themselves and about life.

5. Those who refuse to have a vision for their future

There are many very talented and anointed people I have been in relationship with who live their lives without any strategic plan or vision for their future. They are just living from day to day to prepare for retirement. Those who are successful have a compelling vision that drives them daily and which feeds their souls even more than the desire to make money. Inside of every believer is a God-given Kingdom vision for their future. If a person refuses to tap into that as their guiding light—and value that vision as their barometer for success—then my continual pep talks will not do the trick either!

6. Those who live in self-deception

There are many people who are living lives of denial regarding their relationship with God, their families, and all things regarding their inner and outer lives. The sad thing is that denial is the first step to outright deception. In such a state, a person concocts an alternate, false reality that continually feeds their mind and emotions the things they want to hear about themselves and their key relationships. This insulates them from the Word of the Lord, from others, and the Holy Spirit. When you confront people like this they become upset and blame you for not understanding them, or for wrongfully accusing them of something. These people I cannot help unless God steps in and delivers them from demonic deception (2 Timothy 2:23-25).

7. Those who do not want to pay the price for success

There are many in the church who want the perks of success but don't want to pay the price for success.

When I was a teenager I had a goal of becoming a master guitar player. For seven years I practiced the guitar for 3 to 8 hours per day as well as playing in numerous bands. While my friends were outside playing ball or wasting time doing drugs, I would shut myself up in my house and study jazz, rock, blues, and classical music. I would spend hours doing scales on my guitar (which I often did even while watching television). Because of this sacrifice, I gained mastery over my instrument in various kinds of music and was in high demand as a musician.

Whatever we do in life, we are called to sacrifice our time, invest our talents, and be committed to a long, grueling process with many setbacks until we reach our peak performance. This kind of sacrifice is needed in every area we desire success in, including our marriages, relationships with our children, or leading a company or a church.

Consequently, I have found that I am not able to empower a person to the fullness of their destiny if they don't want to work hard at self-improvement.

8. Those whose primary agenda is individualistic and not Kingdom-oriented

There are some people whose only agenda in life is to advance their own agenda. They don't want to work with a team or flow in the context of a local church. They want me to pour my life into them, but they are rarely ever willing to pour back into the church and serve in the Kingdom of God. I have learned that those who only want to use the church or God to advance their own agendas (even if it is ministry-related) have greatly limited their own lives. Thus, I back away from these people until they change. This is because we are all called to seek first God's Kingdom, in which we need to die to our individualistic sense of destiny and sacrifice and invest our time for the good of the body of Christ. This in turn will do more to release our greatest destiny even more than if we only concentrate on our own agendas!

9. Those who refuse to keep covenant

I have been with very talented individuals with great calling on their lives whom I had to back away from because they did not know how to remain faithful to their obligations, or because they broke confidence by continually talking behind other people's backs. God says that a person who doesn't keep their word (whatever the cost) and who slanders their neighbor cannot dwell in His tents (Psalm 15:3-4). So who am I to think that this kind of person can dwell in my inner circle for personal development?

10. Those who lack transparency, humility, and integrity

The Bible teaches us to walk in the light as He is in the light (1 John 1:7). It also teaches us to confess our faults to one another and pray for one another that we may be healed (James 5:16). Those who do not admit their faults and confess their sins cannot have the kind of relationship with a mentor suitable for personal growth. It is important for me to have a transparent relationship with those I am mentoring, since a person who conceals their sins from me is not giving me a chance to speak fully into their life and help them in their areas of weakness. Those who want to progress in their spiritual formation have to learn to practice the spiritual discipline of confession of sin (Proverbs 28:13).

As you learn to deal with difficult people, though, don't let their problems distract you from focusing on yourself and your need to develop humility, transparency, and the kind of solid foundation that will enable you to withstand the pressures and challenges of ministry. Rest assured, those challenges will come. In Part II, I address a variety of problems in leadership.

PART II: PROBLEMS IN LEADERSHIP

CHAPTER 10

BIBLICAL STANDARDS FOR LEADERSHIP IN AN AGE OF SCANDAL

IN AN AGE OF an Evangelical church culture that is fraught with scandals, we must continually remind and ground ourselves in the biblical criteria for leadership. Otherwise, we will lose our credibility within our churches and before the world. In addition, every church's board of trustees should insist their pastor be accountable to a higher body of leadership or presbytery. This can aid in steering clear of unnecessary challenges related to ministerial integrity.

There is an urgent need in contemporary Christianity to overhaul our assessment and criteria for leadership. This has been made abundantly clear by all the scandals that continue to take place in the church. Those who attempt to bring correction (like I am doing here) are often accused of being legalists or judgmental. I am not advocating that ministers caught in sexual or ethical sin should step down permanently. But, there needs to be a body of leaders to which fallen ministers are accountable so they may be restored to their ministries after demonstrating true repentance and inner healing.

The following are some of the ethical and ministerial standards as related to priests, kings, and New Testament elders. These are qualifications that we can still apply in principle to today's church.

OLD TESTAMENT STANDARDS

For the Priests (Leviticus 21)

Originally, all the children of Israel were to serve as priests of the Lord (Exodus 19:6). But this privilege was evidently taken away and given to the tribe of Levi after the people turned away from the Lord. Among the many laws related to the standards for the priesthood (which relate to all present saints, according to 1 Peter 2:8-9) are some ministerial and ethical principles that we can allegorically extrapolate (although the actual ceremonial qualifications are no longer relevant).

Standard: They shall not dwell among dead bodies and make themselves unclean (Leviticus 21:11). This has to do with not fellowshipping with folks while they are involved in the works of darkness. (Jesus called unconverted people "dead" in John 5:25, Luke 9:60, and Ephesians 2:1-3.)

Principle: I can't tell you how many Christians I know of who think nothing of going out and partying with the world—getting drunk, listening to ungodly music, gambling, or other worldly pursuits.

Standard: They shall not marry a prostitute or a divorced woman but only a virgin (Leviticus 21:13-15). The basic idea of this passage is this: marriage is not a free-for-all. Priests are commanded to marry women of God without previous marital issues. This is so the priestly class is protected from unnecessary distractions and so they nurture their children in a godly environment.

Principle: Jesus modified this view in Matthew 5:31-32 and 19:8-9 for the Kingdom age of the church when He forbade divorce, except for sexual immorality, and forbade marrying a person divorced for an unbiblical reason. (It is now common in the body of Christ for people to divorce just because they don't get along with their spouse. Jesus strictly forbids this.)

Various laws highlight physical defects (Leviticus 21:17-24). Physical defects or blemishes are related to spiritual deficits that hinder a person from ministering for the Lord. For example, lameness represents those whose walk with God doesn't allow them to minister; blindness represents those who have no discernment and no real revelation of Christ in their lives; those with crushed testicles represent those who are not winning souls or bearing any fruit in their ministries; hunchbacks represent those who are not walking uprightly before the Lord (Proverbs 2:21); and dwarfs represent those who have not grown in stature and maturity in Christ (Ephesians 4:13).

Standards for Kings (Deuteronomy 17:14-20)

While the principles for priests relate to all believers, the standards for kings relate specifically to those serving in church leadership.

Standard: A foreigner who is not your brother may not serve as king (Deuteronomy 17:15). Those serving in leadership positions in the body of Christ must be "born again" and demonstrate clear fruits of salvation.

Principle: Often, churches place people in leadership positions without any assurance of their salvation! This dilutes the church of its effectiveness and power to witness to the world!

Standard: Kings must not acquire many horses for themselves (Deuteronomy 17:16). In the Bible, horses represent strength and pride. Thus, God is warning His leaders not to acquire possessions that symbolize their elitism and raise themselves higher than the people in their congregations. For example, there are church leaders who drive very expensive cars or wear $5,000 suits (even though their congregation is very poor) to show people that God is blessing them above everyone else.

Principle: This goes against the principles of humility and simplicity that Jesus and His apostles modeled in Scripture. God forbids kings from acquiring too many horses because it would cause people to turn back to Egypt, which is a symbol of returning to previous ungodly lifestyles they had before experiencing salvation in Christ. Leaders who need material excess in order to be satisfied in this life will produce people who will also get caught up in materialism. This will turn their hearts away from the Lord and back to the things the world values.

Standard: Kings shall not acquire many wives. God was teaching against polygamy and telling the leaders to go back to the one-wife standard, as found in the union between Adam and Eve (Genesis 2:19-22). Although church leaders in America today don't practice polygamy (having more than one legal wife at the same time), more and more leaders in the church are violating the spirit of this passage because they get married, divorced, and remarried numerous times. This is causing unrest, disgust, and alarm among many leaders (including myself) in the body of Christ.

Principle: Ever since the 1980s, when certain national ministers began divorcing and remarrying without adultery or infidelity being cited as the reason (and then on television telling the world that they are blessed), the standards of church leadership regarding marriage and divorce have been sliding down into an abyss.

Several years ago, two high-profile church pastors/leaders divorced. The reasons they gave had nothing to do with adultery but everything to do with simply not getting along or having different visions for ministry. If this is so, they have set an awful example for younger leaders and their congregations by putting their ministry aspirations (or career aspirations) ahead of their marriage vows, which are emblematic of Christ and the church and should never be broken (Ephesians 5:25).

This is different than some of the cases in which a spouse does not want to serve the Lord anymore or wants their spouse to choose between them and the ministry. This is a difficult situation, especially if a person thinks that by resigning they are putting the fleshly desires of their spouse before God.

Standard: Kings shall not acquire for themselves excessive silver or gold (Deuteronomy 17:17). There are some contemporary Christian leaders who live lavishly and receive an inordinate amount of compensation from their churches. I have no problem with a pastor receiving a decent salary, commensurate with their hard work and the size of their church, so they can devote their time to ministering to the church and not be distracted by having to work another job. But some go overboard and live like narcissistic celebrities! This has become a stench in the nostrils of the world and is something that must be adjusted or we will see the judgment of God visit the church like never before!

(I have several income streams related to various aspects of my ministry outside of our local church, so I don't put an excessive burden on the finances of our congregation. Also, I have no issue with someone making a lot of money from book sales, audio sales, and royalties. This is different than making millions in salary from a local church.)

Standard: Kings shall both write and read the Word of God all the days of their lives (Deuteronomy 17:18-19). Christian leaders are required by God to be "People of the Book." We are to focus on the Scriptures, understand all the important doctrines of the church and the Bible, and be able to apply all of this to our personal lives, families, churches, and the surrounding culture.

Principle: There are many leaders who know the sports pages, current events, or the musings of Wall Street more than they know and understand the Scriptures. If we are going to get back to correct standards of holiness, ethics, and ministerial protocol, we need to recapture the simplicity of the gospel (the *kerygma*) and the teachings that apply it (the *Didache*).

Standard: The hearts of kings shall not be lifted up above their brothers. When I was consecrated as a bishop in 2006, many congratulated me for being "elevated." I would cringe when hearing this because I could not picture the Lord Jesus telling His apostles that they were elevated! He told them they were servants, called to wash the feet of the people (John 13).

Principle: When we view leadership as a position, title, or status above others in our faith communities, we are missing the mark of the high calling of God in Christ Jesus and are acting like the world. The world has leaders who lord their authority over their subjects. This is the opposite of what Jesus taught His apostles (Mark 10:42-45).

NEW TESTAMENT CHURCH ELDERS (1 TIM. 3:1-7)

Elders in local churches are those who have the greatest responsibility for leading their congregations. Elder is the highest governmental office in the church—something even the Apostle Peter claimed for himself (1 Peter 5:1). (The fivefold ministry, as found in Ephesians 4:11, describes a function, not an office, of the church.)

Because of the great responsibility, there are some general guidelines that all pastors, fivefold ministers, trustees, deacons, and elders must meet before they are installed. The following is a brief summary:

- They must be above reproach. This regards not having hidden "skeletons in the closet" or a lifestyle that others could seize on and use as an accusation to discredit them.
- They must be the husband of one wife. This has to do with barring a person from serving as an elder who is married to more than one woman at a time. We can also extrapolate from this standard that one should not serve as an elder if they divorced their wife and remarried for anything but the biblical reason of adultery. (However, a case can be made that divorce is acceptable if one's spouse is a violent abuser who threatens their life. But, some would say you could divorce but not remarry in a case like this. There is too much to say regarding this subject to fit in this chapter.)
- They must be sober-minded. This means elders should be serious about the primary things in life related to God, the church, family, and eternity. Their values and priorities should be on things above (Colossians 3:1-3).
- They must be self-controlled. This means a leader needs to live a prudent, discreet life of self-control in which they are not giving in to their fleshly desires or the whims of their physical and sensual passions regarding lust of the flesh, food, and sexual appetite.
- They must be respectable: a person who is not disorderly, but lives a quiet life as a respectable citizen.
- They must be hospitable. Elders should have their marriages, families, and finances in order, to the point where they are able to put up people in their homes as the Lord leads. They should also have people over for dinner.

I know some leaders who never allow anyone near their homes or personal lives. This makes me wonder what they are trying to hide. Hospitality is an important requirement because it enables the discipleship or mentoring process, so those being discipled can go to the next level beyond what is available in larger congregational meetings.

- They must be able to teach. Elders have to be capable of communicating the gospel to the unsaved and applying it practically in a teaching setting for a congregation. Having a Word ministry is an important requirement of all elders.
- They cannot be drunkards. It is not a sin to drink alcoholic beverages, but it is a sin if it becomes a habit and causes drunkenness. This can also be applied to any mind-altering substance.
- Some leaders have become addicted to painkillers, drinking, and other activities that dim the brain to avoid dealing with the pain and pressures of life.
- They must not be violent. Unfortunately, there are many leaders with a violent temper. A violent temper disqualifies a person in God's eyes for eldership in the body of Christ.
- They must not be quarrelsome. There are some leaders who are very argumentative because they have issues in their own hearts that have not been dealt with. While we don't want "yes men" to serve as elders (people who just rubber-stamp everything the senior pastor says without honest dialogue and feedback), we also don't want people serving as elders who must debate everything.
- They must not be lovers of money. Leaders whose hearts are fixated on money are not qualified to be elders because they will always view their ministries and associations with people with a "What's in it for me?" mentality.

Those with serious financial challenges should not serve as elders or trustees because they will be tempted by a conflicting interest when they have business meetings and discuss how to dispense or spend church finances.

- They must manage their households and have their children subject to them. If a person cannot lead their own family, the Bible teaches they cannot manage or lead the household of God. This also means that young children of elders who are still living in their homes should be submissive, attend church, and not be a disruption to the family goal of serving the Lord.
- They must not be a recent convert. In New Testament times, a person had to be at least 30 years old and a believer for several years before they were appointed as elders. This is to protect new converts who could be puffed up with pride if they are put in a position of influence.
- They must have a good reputation with those outside the church. We are not called only to be an example within the church but also outside the church. This is why an elder should not have bad credit, or have a bad record on their job, or a bad reputation among their neighbors.

These are all simple guidelines. Unfortunately, we need to be continually reminded of the first principles and foundational things of leadership so our standards will glorify God and enable us to serve as salt and light in our communities.

THE DARK SIDE

I will conclude this chapter with a checklist of 25 things I use as a reference to be aware of when seeking to adhere to a biblical standard of leadership. Like all human beings, pastors have to guard against operating out of their dark side (false self). Since this is such a salient, direct list, there is no need to elaborate on these 25 signs that indicate you are operating out of your dark side:

1. You inwardly celebrate when a colleague or fellow minister falls.

2. Your spirit of competition causes you to inwardly celebrate when other organizations or ministries in your field aren't doing as well as you.
3. You are more concerned about your local church or organization than the good of the Kingdom of God and cultural transformation.
4. You manipulate people to promote yourself and try to make things happen instead of allowing God to open doors and promote you.
5. You look for opportunities to backstab other leaders in your region or field of work.
6. You are driven to succeed to counter your insecurity, poor self-esteem, and sense of insignificance.
7. You thwart the emergence of other strong leaders in your organization.
8. You are closed-up relationally and have no open, transparent relationships in which you share your weaknesses and fears.
9. You do not share power but work on your own in regard to major decisions that impact your organization or ministry.
10. You are shifty in relationships, taking sides with those you are presently with, and then taking another point of view when with another person when there is a conflict or controversy.
11. You will sacrifice the future for the present in regard to debt-financing and risk-taking instead of leaving a legacy of financial sustainability.
12. You do not receive correction kindly but always get inwardly defensive.
13. You are constantly blaming others when things go wrong.

14. You constantly justify yourself instead of facing your failures.
15. You have no deep relationship with God and lead out of your flesh and soul life.
16. You don't lead by sound biblical principles unless it is convenient.
17. You view yourself more as a pragmatist than a principled person.
18. You are loyal to people only until you have used them to get to the next level.
19. You avoid confrontation and walking in the light according to Matthew 18:15-17 and 1 John 1:7.
20. You only care for those who care for you and serve your agenda.
21. Your greatest desire in life is to make a name for yourself.
22. The bottom line in regard to organizational effectiveness is more important to you than people.
23. You have a hard time forgiving those who offend you.
24. You carry resentment and baggage from the past that you refuse to let go.
25. You don't walk in the peace of God but in the stress of the world.

Just as pastors and leaders need to be aware of the biblical standards of leadership, they also need an understanding of the warning signs that are present before a leadership failure—a topic I review in the next chapter.

CHAPTER 11

WARNING SIGNS BEFORE LEADERSHIP FAILURE

UNFORTUNATELY, IN EVERY LEVEL and realm of life, we have all witnessed serious leadership failure. It is no longer a surprise when we read about a high-level pastor, celebrity, sports figure, or politician who has been disgraced because of ethical or moral failure.

As one who has worked with many struggling church and marketplace leaders on a very personal level since I began serving the body of Christ apostolically in the early 1990s, I have made the following observations regarding warning signs before a fall—which I teach to younger leaders so they will avoid the mistakes of the present generation of many leaders.

All of us have fallen into one of the following in a particular way, shape, or form. Hopefully, we will have learned the hard leadership lessons of life so we can pass on wisdom to the next generation. Here are seven warning signs that precede leadership failure:

1. Busyness

Often before falling a leader will cram so much into his or her schedule for a prolonged amount of time that they don't get enough time for personal renewal and rest. Much activity doesn't necessarily mean Kingdom productivity. When a person is constantly running around from meeting to meeting, from state to state, and from event to event without seeking God and personal times for reflection, they do violence to their soul. They will eventually be operating on willpower and fumes instead of the Spirit of God. This can lead to them being tempted to escape from the pressure of life with adulterous relationships, pornography, excess entertainment, or foolish endeavors.

Activity without clarity will also lead to making poor decisions. When we are always in a rush, we will not have the proper time to process things, which leads to a lack of discernment and disastrous leadership decisions. This will compound the pressure even more and create more work to get out of the mess they are in. Sometimes less is more!

I am not saying that leaders shouldn't be very busy or have a lot of responsibility. What I am saying is there always has to be enough time between events and days of meetings for daily reflection, prayer, and seeking God so that our level of discernment is high. We must walk in the grace and power of God to do His work, instead of our own willpower and strength.

2. Isolation

I have noticed that before falling a leader avoids intimate contact with their peers or overseers who can speak into their life. They live a life of isolation, which is very dangerous!

As busy as I am, there are a number of mentors and spiritual sons whom I open up to who give me input and prayer; I am always open to hearing God's voice through their prayers or exhortations. The more responsibility I have, the more community I need to keep myself on track.

We also need intimate relationships to keep the human side of us active. It is very easy to go from one productive business meeting or anointed service to another and always be in front of strangers, crowds of people, or with leaders who don't know us well. There is no real community in those settings; even in the midst of a crowd, we can isolate ourselves. In a crowd, a leader doesn't have to be intimate or accountable since they are the ones calling the shots and doing the leading and speaking, instead of the other way around.

3. Neglect of family

A leader is heading for a fall when he or she is not spending adequate time with their spouse and/or family. God told us that it is not good for man to be alone. I have seen many leaders, especially those who travel a lot, who are not in regular touch with their spouses and who rarely ever spend time at home. Being with family helps keep a leader grounded. Without that, they will be surrounded by superficial relationships related only to their productivity as a minister or businessperson, where they are always receiving accolades (often from sycophants), as opposed to being a father, mother, husband, or wife who has to constantly strive to work hard at intimacy in their family relationships—which God intended for us to keep us humble and grounded. A leader may get praise from everyone around him (or her), but the spouse really knows them and will tell it like it is and keep them in touch with reality!

4. Lack of self-control

Leaders are heading for trouble when they don't exercise self-discipline in eating and indulging their pleasures. If a leader cannot control their eating patterns, most likely that is a reflection of a larger issue; that is, they are medicating themselves with food and most likely are vulnerable to other lusts of the flesh that will enable them to escape from the pressures of reality. Obesity is a social sin that has become acceptable in the body of Christ even though Jesus warns against it (Luke 21:34).

Furthermore, when we as leaders have bad diets it begins to affect our minds, emotions, and spirits in negative ways. This creates sluggishness and fatigue, and clouds our spirits with carnality. Many leaders have died or have serious health issues once they hit their 40s and 50s because of a poor diet. God will judge us if we prematurely meet Him and miss half our lives because of our lack of discipline and obedience.

5. Spiritual dryness

Leaders are heading for trouble when they don't seek God for God, Himself, only praying and reading the Bible when they have to preach a sermon or minister. Worse than our lack of intimacy with the Lord is the fact that we are only using Him to make a living or using His Word to achieve certain outcomes. However good they may be, our highest call in life is to know and love God. Matthew 7:22-23 teaches us that we can minister for God effectively and still fail if He doesn't know us! Leaders who only seek God for a sermon have a professional relationship with the Lord and will eventually not have the grace and spiritual power to deal with all the pressures of marriage, life, and ministry, which can lead to moral failure.

6. Pride

Leaders who love titles, positions, recognition, constantly join boards, and get involved in large events—all to achieve public prominence—are heading for a fall unless they repent. When we exalt ourselves, God says He will humble us (Luke 14:11), and he who seeks his own glory will not find glory (Proverbs 25:27).

We are not far from a fall when we try to lift ourselves up, promote ourselves, or get involved in events without hearing from the Lord; we are then like the Pharisees, who loved titles, prominent positions, greetings in the marketplace, and to be called leader, reverend, bishop, or doctor (Matthew 23:6-7). Leaders who are broken have learned not to try to create names for themselves by marketing their accomplishments and creating hype; they have learned that only when God exalts a person does it really last (Psalm 75:6).

7. Using people versus empowering them

When leaders use people as objects for their businesses or ministries, instead of having a motivation of empowering people to walk in their purpose—when leaders put programs over people and tasks ahead of relationships—eventually they will have no one around them who is loyal or who they can trust. They will have burned many bridges behind them because, eventually, their followers will become weary of them and leave them. Leadership is a lonely road to walk; leaders more than anyone else need to minister to people with a servant's heart. When leaders come into the ministry with the attitude of being served instead of serving others they develop an entitlement mentality that can lead them to pride, arrogance, and eventually to destruction.

May God help all of us who serve the Kingdom as leaders to glory only in knowing Him (Philippians 3:7-11; Jeremiah 9:23-24)! It is only in following Christ's example and seeking to serve others that we can avoid the inclination to grasp for power and influence. In the next chapter, I will review the signs of power-hungry leaders.

CHAPTER 12

SIGNS OF POWER-HUNGRY LEADERS

GOD-ORDAINED PUBLIC SERVICE should never be about a person's desire for power and prestige, but should arise out of a servant's heart to meet the needs of the people they represent. Jesus modeled this when He washed the feet of His disciples and when He said that the greatest in the Kingdom of God are those who serve (John 13 and Mark 10:43). Of course, we have power-hungry leaders in every sector of society—not just in politics—and this includes the church.

I believe power-hungry people in general are the cause of numerous problems and divisions within the marketplace and church, and we need to be honest with them and speak into their lives when necessary, lest they sabotage great organizations. Since their drive for power to achieve their ends will stop at nothing, more mature leaders need to counter their dangerous ambitions, instead of continually feeding into them. Following are some signs of power-hungry leaders:

(I believe that all leaders, because of our fallen nature, have to deal with some or all of the following issues at times in our lives. But some have totally given in and live out these issues as a lifestyle of choice.)

1. They only relate to other "power" people

Power-hungry people are constantly going to social events, parties, and conferences, and frequently join boards of powerful organizations that will connect them with the most influential people—irrespective of whether they truly have the time and talents, or genuinely want to connect with these people on a human-covenantal level. They are always looking for the next person who can do something to help them climb the social ladders in their spheres of influence, which causes them to use people instead of serve people.

2. They are constantly dropping names and speaking about their accomplishments

There are certain leaders whom I have heard speak several times; every single time they have spoken, either to me in private or in public gatherings, they mention prominent academic institutions where they received their degrees, or drop the names of high-level leaders to whom they have access. After a while it becomes obvious they are attempting to flaunt their power and accomplishments so they can receive accolades or respect from others, instead of it being a sincere attempt to give their audience context for their life narrative.

3. They are in competition with other peer leaders

Power-hungry leaders are always jockeying for position, fighting with other leaders they deem a threat to their influence, or are attempting to marginalize others with faint words of praise or outright gossip and slander. (Immature

Christian leaders usually don't engage in outright slander, but tend to marginalize others subtly when in the company of those they don't know well.) Essentially, power-hungry leaders will not rest until they become the "Big Dog" in the organization.

4. They are all things to all people

Power-hungry leaders often are like chameleons that adapt to the color of their environment. For example, I have met political leaders who speak as biblical Christians when they are speaking in churches, but when they are with secular humanists they speak about their anti-biblical values.

The only thing power-hungry people value is their own power. When they are with Christians they speak religious lingo, and when they are with secularists they speak secular lingo. I don't think even they know what they truly believe!

Unfortunately, many sincere Christians get fooled by these people's surreptitious words and believe anything they hear. After such people are elected, these Christians are shocked by what they really stand for.

5. They are driven by selfish ambition instead of love for people

Though they may work many hours visiting their communities and churches, and being among their people, their ultimate goal is to be in power, not to meet the needs of the people. This is more obvious when it comes to candidates for elected office. But pastors and church leaders have also fallen into this trap and act this out in the context of their own denominations or congregations.

6. They love the praises of men

At the end of the day, power-hungry people live to hear other people sing their praises. They have such low self-esteem that they need to continually feed their egos by being the center of attention at every event, party, and gathering they attend.

Consequently, they are easily insulted when they deem others as not bowing down to kiss their rings sufficiently. They can quickly turn on these people.

7. They often compromise their ethical values

Whatever ethical values they have go out the window if they believe it will help them get into a position of power. For example, some prominent political leaders in our nation (former Vice President Al Gore and Senator Kirsten Gillibrand, to name a couple) were once pro-life when it comes to abortion, but turned pro-choice when they thought it would help them gain traction in their political party. Also, I know of a prominent pastor who once believed in the inspirational integrity of Scripture, but jettisoned his biblical beliefs when he became the senior pastor of a prominent, historic landmark church. What good is your position of power if you are not going to follow your convictions of right and wrong?

8. They have few boundaries to maintain personal and family health

Power-hungry people are constantly on the go and have very little time for personal reflection, renewal, or emotional health. Furthermore, they often are so driven that they cheat their spouses and children out of the precious quality time their family needs. They are always on the phone cutting deals, solving problems, and trying to accomplish the next big thing!

9. They are only loyal to themselves

Power-hungry people are narcissists who have a need to control their environment, their friends, and their futures, which means that ultimately they are only loyal to one person: themselves! They only have people in their inner circles who flatter them and never challenge their egos. They usually don't have close friends, hobnobbing mostly with other power people. In such associations, both people know they are merely using one another to obtain or maintain their power.

10. They head up organizations for stature rather than service

They will go from one church to another, or one position to another, based on which organization will give them the largest platform and most influence. It is never about God's calling but more about influence, public exposure, and proximity to power.

Money is another important issue to them; however, they deem position and influence as more important than money because they believe in the long run more influence will bring in more money anyway!

11. They exaggerate their value

When I am with power-hungry people, I usually take every word they say regarding their influence and accomplishments with a grain of salt. Their main objective is to impress me rather than give me an accurate picture of their lives. For example, I have been with leaders who told me about how large their organizations are, but I have never seen them able to draw a crowd of people anywhere near the numbers they tout. They have erected a symbolic house of straw that they tout as if it were the new Freedom Tower that stands in lower Manhattan!

12. They have a superficial inner life

Power-hungry people usually live in denial as to their real motives and, thus, usually do not allow the searing hot conviction of the Holy Spirit to operate in their souls.

Consequently, they do not have much of a prayer life, do not enter into deep worship, and rarely read the Scriptures—except if they need to put a sermon together or quote passages for a political speech. Furthermore, they attempt to use God for their own ends instead of dying to self and serving God for His own ends and glory. Many actually are so deceived they think God is playing this game with them and is actually empowering them to get more and more attention and power. Little do they realize that Satan is also involved in their lives and setting them up for a huge failure or fall in the future, which can decimate their lives, families, careers, and organizations.

May the Lord help us all to see the above issues we are all grappling with. May all of us be honest with ourselves and our God so we can be delivered from our unholy ambitions and lay down our crowns at the feet of Jesus.

May we also avoid the trap of seeking such power and influence that we become the worst of leaders: abusive, domineering, and controlling people who personify the old adage "My way or the highway!" That is the subject of the next chapter.

CHAPTER 13

SIGNS OF ABUSIVE LEADERSHIP

"For this reason I am writing these things while absent, so that when present I need not use severity, in accordance with the authority which the Lord gave me for building up and not for tearing down" (2 Corinthians 13:10, NASB).

OVER THE PAST SEVERAL decades, there have been many media reports about leaders accused of taking advantage of other people. There is a common pattern of abuse in which leaders use their positions of authority to take advantage of their subordinates or those looking to them for help. There are many signs of abusive leadership, which can relate to leadership in the family, church, business, politics, and/or any organization or voluntary association. Also, often abusers, themselves, are the victims of abuse. The following are characteristics and traits of abusive leadership (Abusive leaders can have one or many of the following traits.):

1. An abusive leader uses his position of power to receive favors from his subordinates

Whenever leaders throw around their title with subordinates to extract personal favors, their motives are impure and these favors can become increasingly illicit. For example, a pastor can pressure a person in their congregation who works in a car dealership to give them a huge discount on a new car, or a CEO can pressure a secretary for sexual favors. The list goes on and on. Unfortunately, often subordinates and/or mentorees want to play the game as much as their leaders to satisfy the underling's quest for success. (In that case, both are equally wrong.)

2. An abusive leader threatens and/or manipulates subordinates to get what they want

When abusive leaders don't get what they want, they often resort to political, monetary, or relational manipulation to coerce their subordinates into submission. When this doesn't work, they often threaten to carry out actions detrimental to the family, career, or life of their subordinate to force compliance. For example, if a boss doesn't get what they want from an employee, they may threaten them by telling them they will not get a much-deserved promotion, or they may pit one person against another in the organization so that they (the boss) can have more political leverage.

3. An abusive leader uses their title primarily for entitlements rather than to serve others

An abusive leader often desires positions of power so they can be served. They want the perks of their position without giving a commensurate sacrifice for those under their auspices. They love the influence and power that comes with their position; this is always dangerous and can lead to leadership abuses. Contrary to this attitude, Jesus taught that the greatest in His Kingdom is not the one who is served but the one who serves (Luke 22:24-27).

4. An abusive leader attaches themselves to the most vulnerable in their midst

Abusive leaders often stay away from smart, confident, independent subordinates who are able to think and take care of themselves. They prey upon the naive, the vulnerable, and/or the stargazers who will do anything to have access to power. Leaders who elevate the vulnerable in their company but shy away from confident individuals with strong core values demonstrate that their desires are to control and manipulate others more than to develop and mature them.

5. An abusive leader uses "father wounds" in others to gain paternal trust

In a world rampant with family fragmentation, a large percentage of people in organizations have an orphan spirit and/or father wounds (as a result of their biological father's neglect and/or abandonment). Abusive male leaders can easily discern this need for paternal affirmation and utilize this felt need in subordinates to take advantage of them. They first gain their trust by showing them attention to earn their loyalty, and then eventually elicit sexual or other favors from them as an expression of some sort of perverse paternal bond with them.

6. An abusive leader makes subordinates inordinately dependent on the leader while isolating them

An abusive leader often makes vulnerable subordinates monetarily, relationally, and/or emotionally dependent on them by taking care of their needs. Their goals are to isolate subordinates so they can continue to control them and extract from them whatever they desire.

7. An abusive leader demands absolute loyalty

Abusive leaders do not want their subordinates or mentorees to receive help or instruction from anyone else. They demand absolute authority and feel threatened when, or if, their subordinates go to anyone else for counsel or aid.

8. An abusive leader threatens and/or attempts to scandalize those who don't comply with their demands

Abusive leaders slander those who turn away from them or those they can no longer control. If they see that a person is, or becomes, self-aware and/or independent and refuses to "drink their Kool-Aid," they slander them and try to limit their ability to succeed without the leader.

9. An abusive leader uses and objectifies others for their own agenda

An abusive leader views others merely as a means to an end to satisfy their personal agenda. They don't value people for who they are, but objectify them to extract from them things the leader desires for themselves. Once the abusive leader gets what they want from a person, they ignore them and go on to the next person they perceive can help them.

10. An abusive leader gets violent and exhibits rage when they don't get their own way

Often an abuser has a short fuse and goes into fits of rage to intimidate their subordinates. If a person has a leader who attempts to elicit obedience through the use of threats, they should disassociate themselves as soon as possible or they may become co-dependent and complicit with the abuser's abuse of others.

11. An abusive leader is narcissistic and focused only on self-gratification

Some leaders attempt to use their position merely as a means for satisfying their ego. They use their position to satiate selfish desires, enjoy a lifestyle of consumerist idolatry, and act narcissistic while not caring about the well-being of subordinates. This myopic and obsessive self-focus always leads to sacrificing others for the sake of their own aggrandizement and pleasure.

12. Abusive leaders are control freaks

Abusive leaders freak out when those in their family and/or organization do not bow down to their every demand. These "control freaks" are motivated by insecurity and fear; they try to create followers in their own image and likeness. They demand predictability, obedience to the status quo, and squash critical thinking, creativity, and independence. They would rather have robotic obedience that produces mediocrity rather than flourishing family members and/or subordinates who fly like eagles.

In conclusion, God gives dire warnings to leaders who only care about themselves to the neglect of those they are supposed to serve (Jeremiah 23:1-4 and Ezekiel 34:1-10). Effective leaders understand that the main reason why they have been entrusted with influence is to facilitate growth and maturity in the lives of those under their care.

Despite the pain involved with the abusive leader, we can learn much about the pitfalls of leadership and how to avoid the systemic problems that can arise from vesting too much power and too little accountability in the hands of one person. In chapter 5, I will delve into these lessons.

CHAPTER 14

LESSONS LEARNED FROM HIGHLY-PUBLICIZED FALLS

Although I first wrote about the resignation of a noted megachurch pastor in the fall of 2014, the issue of overbearing leadership flared into the headlines again recently, when the elders of a well-known megachurch fired their pastor. The latter situation is still playing out; after the pastor's departure several elders indicated they would also step down because of their failures to provide adequate leadership and oversight. In the aftermath of these highly-publicized and contentious situations, many will get caught up in a finger-pointing, "he said, she said" routine, but fail to learn the kind of lasting lessons that will prevent similar scenarios from erupting in the future.

It is interesting to me that, during the past decade, it has been becoming increasingly common for lead pastors to step down from the pulpit for issues other than sexual immorality or financial misdeeds. The reasons vary, but sometimes have to do with arrogance, abusive behavior, or personal issues related to mental and emotional health. This indicates a new and important trend in leadership expectations since, in the past, well-known ministerial leaders would only step down for the scandalous sins of adultery, financial fraud, and other so-called "big sins."

I have followed the story of the challenges related to the leadership style of many of these who have resigned or otherwise been discharged from their church. The following are important lessons we can all learn from these forced separations.

1. There is less tolerance for a top-down leadership style in today's culture

Today's culture is much more egalitarian than in previous generations. In recent decades, most churches and people would have sneezed at the charges laid against some of these leaders, but not anymore. God-glorifying leadership has to go beyond a one-person, autocratic leadership style to one of leading through empowering teams to help accomplish the mission. Strong, secure leaders are not afraid of pushback from other inner-circle leaders, and they enjoy having others involved in the creative process of vision, problem-solving, and execution.

2. There is much more scrutiny today because of social media

In past decades, many of these pastors would still be in their pulpits. However, the times have changed with the advent of the vast social media enterprises that elucidate many of our remarks, as well as spark retorts in the blogosphere. Right or wrong, now everyone in the pew has a voice and they can say whatever they want about their pastors, their sermons, the church, and others via Facebook, Twitter, and other social media platforms.

The result is this: every leader is now living with more scrutiny than ever before in human history. It will only get more intense as time goes on. (This is why every leader should have a social media team to deal with unwarranted and negative things said about them online and in social media.)

3. Love is more important than achievement and results

First Corinthians 13 teaches us the greatest of all attributes is love. God is not impressed with what we accomplish as much as He is interested in why and how we do the things we do. When we objectify the people in our church to get the results we want, we are dehumanizing them and missing the point, even if we seem to get great short-term results.

4. All executive leaders and lead pastors need both internal and external accountability

All too often, elders of churches lack a strong enough voice to stop their pastor from an abusive leadership style. When the internal structure of accountability fails and/or if an elder team cannot stop their leader from deleterious behavior, then the elders should have an outside overseer to confront their lead pastor. There always has to be several layers of recourse in an organizational infrastructure to deal with malfeasance or toxicity in the corporate culture and/or leader.

5. The church often elevates gifted people who are not emotionally mature

Over and over again I see Christian churches and organizations elevating people who are emotionally broken or immature merely because they have great charisma, preaching, or singing ability. All of us have to grapple with the fact that at times our talent can outpace our level of spiritual formation and character. Not every popular preacher is an emotionally healthy and mature Christ-follower.

6. When we do not build on character and integrity our foundation is built on sand

We need to build our lives on the foundations of character and integrity, not on our gifts and talents. Jesus speaks about the Beatitudes before He calls us to be the salt of the earth and the light of the world (Matthew 5:1-16). A life built on gifts and talents without commensurate integrity and character will not finish well. It is a train wreck waiting to happen.

7. There are no shortcuts to success

True success in God's kingdom comes through the grind of brokenness, forged through difficult interactions with people and dealing with circumstances beyond our control. This takes place so that the leader will learn to trust God who alone can redeem our messes so that we can have a powerful message that comforts other people (2 Corinthians 2).

Anytime a leader and or church attempts to circumvent the organic processes of life, experience, transition, change, and crisis (They usually either attempt to exert too much control over others and micromanage or attempt high-risk endeavors that promise a great reward—like a financial scheme.), the endeavor usually fails and causes scandal. God has determined that everyone of us—including leaders—must take up our cross, which has to precede resurrection, to break our will and enable God to empower us with His Spirit.

8. Know who your true friends are before the crisis hits

Too often leaders hit a wall, lose their influence, and find out they have few friends who will stand with them and help restore them. One important lesson here is to identify leaders and friends who love you for who you are and do not need (nor desire) your influence and power. These are the only ones who will love you unconditionally if the day comes when you are in a vulnerable place. Woe to the one who falls and has no one to pick him up (Ecclesiastes 4:10).

9. Leaders must prioritize spiritual formation in the midst of a busy schedule

One of the ways the enemy gets us to fall is to get us so immersed in the "Lord's work" that we neglect our walk with the

Lord. There are times when I am so busy that it is harmful to my soul. When we do not have a sacred rhythm in our lives with times of regular Sabbath and renewal, we are not allowing God to have space in our lives to bring inner transformation. This will eventually lead to burnout and a career crash.

10. It is not how you start but how you finish that matters most

Many young leaders have started out well, with amazing church growth and popularity. Consequently, thousands of other young leaders are enamored and begin to emulate them and model their lives, ministry, and doctrine on them. I learned a long time ago that we can never judge the ministry or mettle of a man until they go through the fire. Jesus told us that only those who build their house on the Rock will be able to stand once the storms and fiery trials of life hit (Matthew 7:24-27).

In addition to these key lessons, there are others that congregations as well as individuals would do well to grasp as we move into the future. I will address these in the next chapter.

CHAPTER 15

WHAT CHURCHES CAN LEARN FROM OTHERS IMPLODING

NEWS REPORTS SAID IN the aftermath of one megachurch pastor's resignation, that the church lost half of its 10,000-plus attendees. The remaining campuses devolved into independent, autonomous entities with the option of continuing, merging with other churches, or disbanding like the mother church did a few months after the pastor stepped down.

There are lessons we can all learn from this as individuals. More importantly, churches should take heed to how a congregation can implode so easily based on the behavior of a key leader.

(Please note: I recently became acquainted with one of these pastors and have no first-hand knowledge of what transpired at his church. Also, there is another side to the story—as with all stories. The alleged issues he supposedly had—if true—are not uncommon in the church or among leadership in general. In my opinion, many leaders have done far worse and are still in their pulpits.)

Conversely, in the aftermath of another megachurch pastor's resignation several years after the one I mentioned in the previous chapter, and the subsequent resignations of other leaders, board members, and pastors, the church has been hobbling. However, as of the writing of this book, it is still standing.

There's a reason I'm not using any names or places: I don't want to dredge up past failures or stir up any more controversy. Besides, it is more important that we heed the lessons we can learn from these unfortunate church implosions and other, similar experiences that are all too common in the contemporary church world.

The following are seven lessons all churches can learn from these local church implosions:

1. Every lead pastor needs both internal and external accountability

In my opinion, every lead pastor needs to be accountable internally to the board of elders for both spiritual and financial issues of the church. Also, a lead pastor should always attempt to function with the consensus of both the elders and trustees, especially when it comes to major financial decisions. Furthermore, every lead pastor needs to have at least one outside local leader to be their overseer and hold them accountable for matters regarding their personal life and family.

It is very difficult, awkward, and often not practical for internal leaders to serve in that role. (It is hard for leaders who the lead pastor has nurtured into eldership to be able to speak into the personal life of their overseer and shepherd. Thus, every shepherd needs an outside voice as their shepherd.)

2. Church elders need an apostolic overseer to appeal to in case of an impasse

Often church elders have no one to look to when they reach an impasse with the lead pastor. This is why they vote with their feet, resign, cause division, and/or attempt to start another church. Every church eldership needs to have a person it can appeal to if the elders and lead pastor hit a major wall regarding church governance or personal issues with the lead pastor. This is why I am a major proponent of having an "apostolic church" template, in which every local church is overseen by a lead pastor, who is also submitted to an apostolic leader or bishop who oversees other associated congregations. This is the New Testament pattern and is much better than leaving congregations and leaders all by themselves.

3. Satellite churches need their own pastor/preacher

The satellite (or multi-site) model structure often involves a simulcast of the lead pastor's message to all the other campuses. Thus, while the church is expanding in numbers, it is not always developing leaders commensurate with this expansion. This is dissimilar to church planting in which every congregation has its own lead pastor, preacher, and leadership team. Consequently, every campus is being built around the preaching, leadership, and vision casting of one man—which leaves them vulnerable to the kind of implosion which will scatter all the connected congregations.

4. The "one man brand" of the church leaves the church vulnerable

Most of the time, congregations know their charismatic lead pastor more than their own congregation or vision. At one of the aforementioned megachurches, the pastor was a major part of their "brand." Not only that, but evangelical churches too often perpetuate a personality cult in which folks say something like, "I am going to Joe Mattera's church," rather than, "I am going to Resurrection Church." You get the picture? Many people can't even remember the name of the church they visited; they only know the church by the name of the lead pastor.

This is nothing new. It's the same thing that the Apostle Paul had to address with the Corinthian church (1 Corinthians 3:4). Although this is common with evangelical churches, that doesn't mean it is healthy, and it is something in our present global church culture that must change. One of the things we have done in our church the past decade is to have a team of leaders who rotate and share the responsibility of delivering the Word on Sunday mornings. This is so that people don't just hear the Word from one person. Also, for the past few years we have gone from topical to exegetical teaching on Sundays, so the focus is on understanding the Scriptures rather than the skilled presentation of the lead pastor.

5. The essence of the church needs to be based on the centrality of Christ

Along the lines of point four, there needs to be a drastic shift away from a congregation that comes to be entertained by a great worship leader and/or preacher to a congregation that comes primarily to worship Jesus. Every church has to ingrain its vision, mission, preaching, ministry, and worship around the centrality of Christ. This is one of the advantages some of the historic mainline denominational churches have over the typical evangelical church. In spite of the fact that Roman Catholic, Eastern Orthodox, and other denominational churches transfer their priest every few years to another parish, faithful people still attend their churches by the millions all over the world. Why? Because their congregations are committed to their parish, and to their expression of the universal church, more than they are to the charismatic leadership of their lead pastor.

For example, in my neighborhood in New York City, a Roman Catholic might say, "I am attending Saint Francis church in Brooklyn Heights." They rarely,–if ever–say, "I am attending Father Frank Mascara's church."

One of the reasons I instituted weekly Communion years ago in our church was because I wanted the center of the service to be about the gospel, not about my preaching. When people judge a church merely by good sermons and/or worship experiences they are acting carnal. Their focus should be on worshiping Jesus, ministering to the saints, and being empowered for the work of the Kingdom in the context of the corporate vision of their local congregation.

6. Every lead pastor needs an equally competent understudy who can step in

After some of these incredibly gifted leaders resigned, there was no understudy with a similar capacity to come in and preach (and lead) them. In my opinion, the greatest role of every lead pastor is to nurture leaders who can potentially step into their role and do an even better job.

Of course, as in New Testament times, a church can be led by a team of overseers until the right leader comes along. (The letters of Paul were all written to elders and deacons, as well as the congregation—not to one lead pastor.)

7. The congregation has to be more committed to their corporate vision than to the lead pastor and/or to their social networks

Most people attend a church because a friend attends and/or because they like the lead pastor. We have to structure our churches so that we develop a discipleship culture, in which believers are assimilated to serve their church and community. Folks have to discover their individual gifts and have their purpose ignited with a passion inspired by a compelling corporate vision to transform their city that transcends their social networking needs.

In closing, those of us in the evangelical church will miss an opportunity for growth unless we admit that much of the leadership and character issues that lead to the resignation of lead pastors are common issues with a large percentage of pastors globally. Also, many of the flaws in the structure of churches that have experienced implosions are also fatal flaws in a large percentage of all evangelical churches worldwide. We should allow the Lord to redeem the experience of struggling churches as a teaching moment for us all.

May the Lord minister grace, mercy, and restoration to all pastors and leaders who have either fallen, resigned from the ministry, or experienced burnout and quit. And may the believers who are a part of such congregations not only survive but also thrive in the years ahead for the glory of God.

One way all congregations and their pastors can survive for the long-term is to be aware of the dangerous signs of burnout, which I will review in the next chapter.

CHAPTER 16

SIGNS OF LEADERSHIP BURNOUT

IN MY YEARS OF ministry, I have seen many leaders lose their zeal for God and leave the ministry. Often, this has occurred because they did not take adequate time to seek the Lord on a daily basis for self-renewal. Other reasons include not having a balanced life that incorporates things that advance physical and emotional health. (Instead, they just focus on work and ministry).

I too have been guilty of not taking enough time off, having never taken more than 10 days straight for vacation in all my years of hard, grueling ministry (with 95 percent of my vacations being only 5-7 days long). Until recently, I never took one full day off per week to rest my mind. At this stage of life, I am being forced to change my patterns because I have exhausted much of my mental energy and can no longer cheat. (The main reason I have lasted this long without enough regular time off is because I keep a strict diet, exercise regularly, and spend time seeking God every morning.)

I knew it was time to stop cheating because of some burnout symptoms I came perilously close to experiencing. Over the years, I have done much research on this subject as well as ministered to many leaders suffering from burnout.

The focus of this chapter is not how to recover from burnout, but how to recognize some of the signs of burnout. (I will mention a few points at the end that will aid in recovery.) The following are signs of emotional and mental burnout:

1. You lose focus and clarity of thought

When experiencing burnout, your mind hits a wall and you have fogginess of thought instead of clarity. Sometimes your short-term memory even deteriorates because of the mental overload.

2. You lose your passion for work and/or ministry

You dread going to the office or conducting meetings. Yet you do it because it represents a commitment more than because it is a passion in your life.

3. You go from being a leader to being a maintainer

The primary calling of a senior leader is to be a visionary. Visionaries are at their best when they receive instruction from God at the top of the mountain and then come down and give vision to their congregation or organization. When experiencing burnout, a leader doesn't have the capacity for any more vision. Hence, all forward motion grinds to a halt and the leader goes into maintenance mode. They try their best to hold everything together, desperately hoping they will recover the energy needed to take their organization to the next level.

Unless they take adequate steps for restoration, leaders like this will only get worse, not better. They will begin to see people leaving their church or organization, because unless there is a compelling vision coming from the leader, the people scatter (Proverbs 29:18).

4. You have a continual sense of hopelessness

In burnout your hope for the future grows dim, depression begins to set in, and you begin to view the world with dark, gray lenses because you tend to highlight only the negative in your mind.

5. You isolate yourself from others

When in burnout, you start creating more and more emotional space from others. You lack the emotional and mental capacity to carry on extensive conversations and/or minister to another person's needs.

6. You run from new challenges

A church needs to ensure their lead pastor takes regular sabbaticals. Unless the senior leader goes away for an extended time to renew and refresh themselves every several years, the vision of the church or organization will be limited. That's because the senior leader will begin to shy away from new challenges, new vision, and forward motion. An unrenewed lead pastor will greatly limit the capacity of a church to expand and grow.

7. You don't want to problem-solve

A person in burnout doesn't want to strategize or problem-solve because it takes too much mental energy.

8. You dream more about retirement than taking a mountain

I knew I was starting to get too close to the edge when I kept envisioning the scene in the movie *Gladiator*, when the lead character, Maximus, is about to die, and he keeps envisioning the next life in paradise, when he would rest from war and enjoy life with his loved ones.

When you are dreaming about laying down your weapons instead of going off to war to defeat your foes, then you know it is time to get recharged. Anyone who lives for retirement is a person who has already stopped living. For example, when a lead pastor gets to the place when they are looking at their watch on Sunday because they can't wait until the services end so they can go home and relax, then you know they need to be retrofitted and recharged. God has called leaders to minister out of their abundance and overflow, not from the fumes of an empty tank!

9. You lack patience for all things mundane

Those in burnout lose their patience for all things petty when dealing with relational challenges. (In the past they had grace for the immaturity of the saints, but in burnout they have no patience for it.) They also lack the patience to deal with average things needed to maintain oversight of their staff and organizational business.

10. You view ministry as work rather than a calling

The greatest privilege I will ever have in my life is to represent the Lord Jesus as the overseer of a local church. It is not a job but a calling. When in burnout, sometimes the only thing that stops a pastor or leader from leaving the ministry is economics (their paycheck). The moment I stay in a church for the salary I will have gone from being a shepherd to a hireling. It is not a job, but a holy vocation (1 Corinthians 4:1).

HOW TO RECOVER

1. Honor the biblical Sabbath

Take time away to pray, study, and refresh yourself. Take at least one day off in seven. For pastors, they can't count Sunday as a day off because it is a workday. What has worked for some pastors is to take a weekday off, or from Friday night to Saturday night. (However, Saturday is often spent in sermon preparation, so that may not work for some).

2. Spend time enjoying the Lord on a daily basis

I believe that burnout comes the quickest when we stop spending adequate time with the Lord. Hebrews 4 teaches us that when we enter God's rest we cease from our own labors; when we attempt to lead in our own strength, God allows us to lose our energy because unless the Lord builds the house we labor in vain (Psalm 127).

3. Prioritize the things that are life-giving to you

God has wired each of us so that certain things we do are life-giving, while other things deplete life. For example, being around people energizes extroverts, while introverts are sapped of energy when with people. Introverts need to schedule regular time alone to recharge in order for them to meet the challenges they face daily.

Prioritize time with God and for reading the Bible, church gatherings for spiritual renewal, spending time with key friends, time with family, exercise for physical health, hobbies, and enjoying good music and literature for mental renewal.

4. Recapture your original calling and vision

When lost at sea, a person must read their compass to get back on course. When we lose clarity of vision and focus, we need to read our journals and recapture things God has told us that enable us to recapture our original calling and commission.

5. Stay in accountable relationships with a leadership community

We all need spiritual mentors and spiritual oversight. If you are a pastor, find a pastoral community of leaders in which you can experience peer friendships, coaching, accountability, and covenant. If you are in a local church and you are a leader, attach yourself to the leadership communities that are available to you.

Proverbs teaches us that, as iron sharpens iron, so one man sharpens another. Being in a community can hasten your restoration; isolating yourself from other leaders and from the body of Christ is one of the devil's strategies to destroy us since during fragile times in our lives we need wise input from others more than ever!

In addition to recognizing the signs of burnout, another key to effective ministry comes from awareness of the greatest temptations awaiting leaders in the wilderness—the subject of the next chapter.

Recommended Reading

Leading on Empty: Refilling Your Tank and Renewing Your Passion by Wayne Cordeiro

"Taking a Break From the Lord's Work," by Paul Vitello, *The New York Times,* August 1, 2010

CHAPTER 17

THE GREATEST TEMPTATIONS FOR LEADERS IN THE WILDERNESS

And Jesus, full of the Holy Spirit, returned from the Jordan and was led by the Spirit in the wilderness for forty days, being tempted by the devil. And he ate nothing during those days. And when they were ended, he was hungry. The devil said to him, 'If you are the Son of God, command this stone to become bread.' And Jesus answered him, 'It is written, "Man shall not live by bread alone."' And the devil took him up and showed him all the kingdoms of the world in a moment of time, and said to him, 'To you I will give all this authority and their glory, for it has been delivered to me, and I give it to whom I will. If you, then, will worship me, it will all be yours.' And Jesus answered him, 'It is written, "You shall worship the Lord your God, and him only shall you serve."' And he took him to Jerusalem and set him on the pinnacle of the temple and said to him, 'If you are the Son of God, throw yourself down from here, for it is written, "He will command his angels concerning you, to guard you," and "On their hands they will bear you up, lest you strike your foot against a stone."' And Jesus answered him, 'It is said, "You shall not put the Lord your God to the test."' And when the devil had ended every temptation, he departed from him until an opportune time" (Luke 4:1-13, ESV).

The Gospels of Matthew and Luke both show that the Lord Jesus, the greatest leader the world has ever known, was tempted in the wilderness for 40 days. Since Luke 4:2 actually says that Jesus was tempted for 40 days, the temptations mentioned probably serve more as a summary—or categories—of the various kinds of temptations the Lord went through.

The following are four major temptations all leaders will have when they are in a time of personal testing. We can safely assume that, since these were the four temptations the devil used to tempt Jesus (as the Son of God), these are the most difficult temptations for leaders to avoid or overcome before we have proven ourselves to enter the fullness of our ministry and purpose.

THE FOUR TEMPTATIONS

1. "If you are the Son of God . . ." Satan tries to get us to doubt our identity as children of God.

When Satan put the word "if" in front of "the Son of God" he was attempting to put the seed of doubt inside of Him in regard to His relationship as the Son of God. The number one thing Satan tries to attack when we are in a time of testing is our confidence in our identity with God, regarding our relationship with Him as a son or daughter, and our vocation in the Kingdom. Everything we do in ministry should come out of the fact that we are children of God by faith in Christ Jesus (Galatians 3:26). Ephesians 3:19 says that we as believers in Christ are in the household of God. There is nothing more important to understand and cultivate than this. Even our experiences with the Holy Spirit will first and foremost bear witness that we are God's children in which we cry out from the depths of our heart, "Abba, Father" (Romans 8:16). Abba is an endearing term equivalent to the vernacular "poppa" or "daddy." This is the number one thing the devil will attack since, if he can get you doubting your relationship with God as your father, or your salvation in Christ, he will successfully neutralize your effectiveness on the earth because you have no solid footing!

The second way Satan will attack beside our relationship with the Father is to cause us to doubt our calling into the ministry, or to doubt our effectiveness in ministry. When we are in the wilderness, if Satan cannot get us to doubt our relationship with God, he will then focus on attacking our minds in regard to our calling from God. When we are in the ministry and get tested, it is vital that we remain focused on the word God impressed on our hearts that consecrated us for the ministry. We must stay focused on our purpose. When all else fails and all hell is breaking loose around you, never stop focusing on the destiny God put on the inside of you!

2. ". . . Turn these stones into bread." Satan tries to get us to perform to prove our standing with God as His child.

Satan attempted to get Jesus to perform a miracle in order to prove that He was the Son of God. In the same way that my natural children do not have to do any great work in order to be my son or daughter, I cannot earn my standing with God as His child by performing works.

When someone gets involved with works for salvation or a works mentality in order to please God, they have been sucked into a system built on human pride instead of on God's grace, which is given to us outside of our works (Romans 3:21-31).

Unfortunately, many leaders have fallen into a performance trap in which they attempt to obtain God's favor or love by their ministry or works of service to their community.

Although Christians are called to be involved in good works, the truth is good works do not save us, and we are not earning God's love by our good works. We are first and foremost placed in Christ Jesus as His children by faith, and then we are called to do good works as an expression of the favor and love we have already received from God, not to try to earn that love and relationship! Works should always be based on the overflow God has already freely given to us by His grace. Ephesians 2:8-10 explains the proper relationship and chronology between salvation and works.

3. Satan offers us power without process or pain.

Satan basically attempted to give Jesus a shortcut to fulfilling His purpose of inheriting all the kingdoms of the world, if He would only bow down and worship the devil. Satan offered Him these kingdoms because, having failed to get Jesus to doubt His identity and calling, he then tried to get Jesus to attempt to fulfill His calling of inheriting all the nations of the world without going to the cross and suffering. Basically, he was offering Jesus a "quick fix," or a shortcut to His destiny, that did not involve the cross.

Consider the principle: "If something offered to you is too good to be true, then it probably isn't true or good for you!" Another adage is this: "Without pain, there is no gain." These two adages are true in every area of life, whether it is in the gym, sports, business, education, or politics. These sayings are not just true in Christianity.

The Greatest Temptations for Leaders in the Wilderness

Anyone who preaches that we can have success in life without denying ourselves and putting our flesh on the cross is preaching heresy. Before you get to the fullness of Pentecost, you must first experience the fullness of Golgotha!

God always surrounds power with problems and responsibilities, because God can only trust those who are humble and broken in regard to their will to steward power.

True power with God comes by life processes that involve pain in relationships, overcoming temptation, problem-solving, dealing with crises, time management, prioritizing, and overcoming huge challenges and problems in order to obtain the goals set before us. For example, it wasn't until Jacob walked with a limp that he actually obtained power with God and became a man of God (Genesis 32:24-32).

Humbly going through the crosses of life that serve to crucify the flesh and break our stubborn will is the process that leads to purpose. This is why, when the Apostle Peter tried to stop Jesus from going to the cross, Jesus called him Satan (Matthew 16:23), but when Judas betrayed Jesus and caused Him to be crucified, He called him friend (Matthew 26:50).

4. Satan tried to get Jesus to fall into the sin of presumption. "(The devil) set Him on the pinnacle of the temple, and said to Him, 'If you are the Son of God, throw yourself down from here'" (ESV).

Satan tried to get Jesus to put Himself in harm's way because of a general principle in Psalm 91 that the devil took out of context. Often, leaders under pressure during times of testing get anxious, have knee-jerk reactions, and move ahead of the Lord and make poor decisions because they don't wait on God long enough to discern His will. The sin of presumption is one of the most destructive of all sins.

For example, whenever a person makes huge plans without knowing the specific mind of the Lord in a matter, they are testing God and are guilty of the sin of presumption.

Leaders, no matter how busy, need to spend adequate time before God in prayer, study of His word, and in regular interface with godly people so they are always in a position of hearing the voice of God and/or receiving input from God in one way or another.

I have seen countless leaders making huge declarations—even saying, "Thus says the Lord," regarding big plans they have—resulting in disaster, proving they never actually heard from God and were operating in presumption.

These are four of the major tests all leaders will have. There are many other tests that will come under a subcategory of one of these four macro categories. Truly, these tests the Lord persevered through were not recorded for His sake, but for the sake of all Christ-followers that He has called to transform this world!

In addition to these temptations, pastors of any congregation—whether a megachurch or a rural body of 100 people—can assume so much power and authority while failing to maintain relationships of accountability that they can turn into demigods. Namely, leaders whose word is unquestionable and who demand absolute loyalty is never a healthy situation.

CHAPTER 18

CHARACTERISTICS OF DEMIGOD LEADERS

IN RECENT YEARS THE church has seen the rise of celebrity, cult-status pastors who act like spiritual divas. I define demigods as those who act as little gods and believe they are above everyone else.

These leaders walk around with an entourage and bodyguards, are inaccessible to even high-level staff and peers, and are unaccountable islands to themselves. Furthermore, no matter how much these demigod leaders violate biblical ethics, they still maintain their leadership positions because most of their followers are blinded by devotion.

Many of these leaders started in ministry for the right reasons, but because of unresolved emotional dysfunction—often related to youthful experiences in fragmented families fraught with abuse, neglect, and anger—they carry these dysfunctions over into their ministries and church families.

There are some social and psychological reasons for this aberrant behavior, both from the vantage point of these leaders and their followers. The following are some of these symptoms and reasons:

WHY FOLLOWERS FALL FOR DEMIGOD LEADERS

1. Many Christians come from dysfunctional family backgrounds and need male hero figures to emulate as father figures

Some folks view their Spirit-led leaders as surrogate fathers. Hence they will be protective of their leaders to the point at which their emotional connection and loyalty clouds biblical truth.

2. Many Christians have no identity of their own and live vicariously through their leaders

Those without a healthy self-identity gravitate towards strong, confident leaders with a compelling vision to the point at which their own individuality is subsumed or fragmented. This creates a vacuum of being and essence, which makes them vulnerable to charismatic leaders. For example, this is how false prophet Jim Jones was able to lead 900 followers, including some who were well-educated, into committing corporate suicide in Guyana in 1978.

3. Many have a strong sense of failure and live through the success of their leaders

Many people live boring lives without purpose and feel they have more meaning when vicariously living through a person they deem successful.

4. Many followers lack their own intimate knowledge of Christ and are ignorant of Scripture

Unfortunately, most Christians are biblically-illiterate and will believe anything their leaders teach them, even if it is heretical. Hence, their leaders can live lives or lead their churches in ways that are not congruent with Scripture, and they wouldn't even know it!

5. Many stay connected to their leaders primarily because of their social communities

After being in a church for several years, folks usually assimilate into that particular faith community (which is a great thing in most cases) and build their social networks around their church lives and ministries. If they leave their churches, they will have to cut off many of these social ties. Thus, many will continue in a church even if the leader is living an ungodly life full of pride, abuse, or manipulation.

6. Many are connected to demigod leaders because it gives them religious status

There are many people I have met who attend certain churches only because those churches have many members, even if they are not maturing in the Lord. They remain in these churches because the celebrity status of their leaders gives them status with other Christians in their cities.

7. Many have low self-esteem and don't recognize when they are being abused or manipulated

Those with low self-esteem will allow others to abuse, disrespect, and even manipulate them because they don't have enough self-dignity to disapprove, or even recognize it. Many of these folks were abused or neglected at home and live with a sense of guilt and feel an unconscious need to have authority figures that act the same way as their parents did. (This satisfies their feelings of guilt in some cases.)

WHY LEADERS BECOME DEMIGODS

1. They have a sense of entitlement

Some folks think of themselves more highly than they ought and believe in their hearts that they deserve better treatment than any other human being (Romans 12:3).

2. Because of their celebrity status they think they are above the law

When celebrity leaders (who could be celebrities in small churches as well as large churches, based on the adulation of the people and their own self-deception) get used to having sycophants around them, they become used to getting what they want, when they want it. Hence, they push aside boundaries and live lives that satisfy their fleshly inclinations.

3. They are unaccountable because they don't think anyone is qualified to speak into their lives

Some pastors and leaders think they are so spiritual and successful that they have reached a point where no one is able to speak into their lives and teach them anything. They may ask in their minds questions like, "Is this person as wealthy as me?" or, "Do they have as many people in their church as I do?" before they even consider hearing what others have to say!

4. They are aloof because they don't trust anyone

Many demigod leaders are really projecting a false sense of confidence and aloofness because they don't trust anyone enough to have intimate relationships—including their spouses and children.

5. Their self-identity is subsumed by their ministry identity

Some start off okay, but eventually their success—fueled by their driving ambition to be respected and known—becomes the primary way they view themselves. Thus, they lose their core essence and live through a false sense of success and power.

6. They become narcissistic to medicate the pain of their past

Many demigod leaders abuse their leadership privileges by manipulating others for their own advantages, and/or are involved in substance abuse, adultery, excessive entertainment, frequent vacations, and other lusts of the flesh to medicate their unresolved pain from the great responsibilities, intense life, and other pressure-cooker items that make them feel trapped, with no outlet. Thus, they succumb to temporary fixes that give them a reprieve from their miserable reality.

7. They erroneously believe ministry anointing equates with God's favor

Some believe that because they preach great messages and experience the power of God when ministering that God's favor is on them, even if they are not living lives of holiness.

Scripture teaches us through the life of Samson that, eventually, putting anointing before the fruit of the Spirit and walking with the Lord will catch up with us, and we will miss our destiny or have untimely ends to our ministry effectiveness.

8. They preach Christ without a cross—a gospel centered on self rather than on sacrifice

Some demigod leaders believe and preach a rights-centered gospel that is centered on self rather than on Christ. This results in living lives of indulgence that have no boundaries, which give them limitless desires for the physical amenities of life.

9. They associate with other demigod leaders who reinforce a demigod leadership culture

The old saying, "Birds of a feather flock together," is a truism. People tend to congregate mostly with others who believe like them and reinforce their belief systems and lifestyles, which can either be a force for good or evil.

Demigod leaders tend to associate with other spiritual divas and even have them preach in their churches because they don't want any dissident voices that would call them to account and bring a standard of holiness.

CHARACTERISTICS OF NARCISSISTIC DEMIGODS

Some demigod leaders also can be called narcissists. By definition, a narcissist is a person who believes the world revolves around them to such an extent their own desires blind them to relational reality, which makes them insensitive to the needs and perspectives of others. One of the sad realities in our modern, consumer-driven, hedonistic culture is that we are producing millions of narcissistic people, including leaders of large organizations.

Because of our sinful nature as human beings, all of us have some narcissistic tendencies to deal with. The following traits identify leadership narcissism.

1. When leaders think others are there to serve them instead of vice versa

This reverses the principle in Matthew 20:26-28, in which Jesus says a great person in the kingdom is one who serves and that He didn't come to be served, but to serve and give His life as a ransom for many.

In an organization or church led by a leader of this type, the ladder for success is based more on catering to the narcissism of the leader than on merit or work output. (Note: I am not discounting the importance of loyalty with this statement.)

2. When leaders want the perks of the ministry without the pain of the ministry

There are leaders I know who want titles, prestige, honor, and the respect that comes with a leadership position, but they don't want to pay the price for it. Most successful senior leaders and CEOs already understand this, so this problem is more prevalent among secondary leaders working closely with senior leaders. Such folks desire recognition as a top leader, but don't do the hard work necessary for excellent results.

3. When leaders put their own needs before the needs of the organization they lead

True spiritual leaders give their lives for the sheep in the same way the Lord Jesus did (John 10). Narcissistic leaders will fleece the sheep and financially jeopardize their organizations

Characteristics Of Demigod Leaders

for the sake of their self-indulgent lifestyles. (This is totally contrary to the prophetic warnings to shepherds found in Jeremiah 23!)

4. Leaders who are self-indulgent when it comes to the material things of this world

Some leaders have an excessive desire to continually shop for the things that interest them (clothes, cars, computers, etc.) in order to keep them happy and motivated to serve. Along with this may be an excessive desire for entertainment, pleasure, or play.

5. Leaders who look for close relationships with those who pander to them and avoid those who confront them

Some leaders will only have people in their inner circles who pander to their need to feel superior. They do not want people around them who disagree with them or speak into their lives. These leaders continually fall for flattery, which opens a huge door to Satanic deception.

6. When leaders view people as objects to use for their own advantage

Instead of regarding people as fellow image-bearers of God, some leaders view the importance of people based on if they can serve their agenda. As soon as they believe a person is no longer contributing to their agenda, they begin to ignore them and look for the next person they can use. To this end, they court and even flatter people they have their eyes on, treating them like the most important people in the world, which abruptly comes to a halt when their services are no longer needed.

7. Leaders who are uninterested in other people's problems

Some leaders have no attention span for others while they are speaking about their own issues or problems. They will engage conversations as long as it is about them or something they are interested in, but will shut down emotionally as soon as the conversation shifts to something outside their interests.

8. Leaders who rarely give in to other people's ideas

Some leaders are not good listeners, refuse to bend, and even act emotionally immature when they don't get their way or when an idea of theirs is not acted on or agreed with. Once leaders like this have decided they want something, it is almost impossible to change their minds unless they hear another idea that benefits them even more.

9. Leaders who cannot have intimate emotional connections with close associates or their spouses

Because of a lack of interest in meeting the needs of others, some leaders will only have superficial friendships based on fun, entertainment, and gossip. When conflicts arise, they shy away from relationships since they are no longer meeting their cravings for fun, escape, and entertainment.

Their marriages are great in the beginning, when they are in the honeymoon stage and enjoying a robust sex life. But when the pressures of raising children, finances, and time management kick in, they bury themselves in things that help them escape reality: another relationship, entertainment, hobbies, and the like. Their marriages grow farther and farther apart as they literally become emotionally divorced before the eventual physical divorce takes place (unless, through self-awareness and repentance, their marriages can be saved).

10. Narcissistic leaders are more vulnerable to sexual sins

Narcissistic people are easily bored and are prone to look at pornography and commit adultery because their main desire from sex is not emotional intimacy, but physical pleasure. As soon as the excitement wears off in their relationships, they look for others who can sexually arouse them. In those cases where adultery has not yet occurred, those with a high libido will gravitate to pornography within six months to one year of every serious relationship they are in and in many cases will hide their continual use of pornography throughout every relationship they have.

Furthermore, narcissistic spiritual leaders are easy prey to the flattery of the opposite sex, which leads to adultery—even in churches they oversee. This is because, unless the cross of Christ is directly applied to their deep emotional need to be the center of attention, when their spouse doesn't meet their expectations, they will drift to someone else to meet their addiction to praise.

Embracing the traits of a demigod will lead to serious problems, including the collapse of ministries, personal ruin, and an end to ministerial careers. More importantly, this damages God's name among those in the world. But rest assured, He will not allow such fleshly behavior to continue forever. In the next chapter, I review a prophetic word about coming failures and falls that is as fresh as the day I received it.

CHAPTER 19

HOW THE MIGHTY FALL

SOME TIME AGO, AS I was praying with my dear friend, Lenny Weston (a prophetic pastor residing in Ohio), he sensed the Lord saying to him, *"How the mighty have fallen; I am going to remove many candlesticks from their places, so that the church will trust in Me and not in men. I am going to remove many prominent leaders and rise up many unknown leaders to prominence that will speak for Me. As a result of this, many in the church will be shaken and some will fall away."* Lenny reflected on this prophetic word, "While most in the church are focusing their prayers for the nation because of same-sex marriage and abortion, more believers are needed to pray for the church at this time."

There was more to this word, but those were the main points based on my recollection. Since Lenny has a solid walk with God, I took this word seriously! It may start to be fulfilled very shortly, or it could start in several years. Of course, every year we hear about several prominent Christian leaders falling into sin or being removed from their ministry. The gist of this word seems to indicate that what is coming will be a tsunami compared to what has transpired in the past.

This chapter was triggered by the word Lenny shared with me. I do not presume to understand the timing of this word and/or the methods God may use to fulfill it. However, using biblical principles and having an understanding of the past, I have responded to this word with seven possible reasons the mighty will fall:

1. The authority of Scripture is undermined

In my opinion, God brought a severe correction to the Roman Catholic system with the advent of the Protestant Reformation in the 16th century, because they placed church tradition and their canon law on a higher level than Scripture. As a result, their ecclesiastical structure became corrupted as they adopted unbiblical doctrines: Mary worship; justification by works; idol worship in the church; praying for the dead; praying to the saints; indulgences; purgatory; the office of the pope as the vice regent of God's Kingdom on earth; and transubstantiation. They believe that during Communion the wafer and the wine literally become the body and blood of Jesus, which violates Hebrews 10:10-14, which teaches that Jesus only had to make one sacrifice for all time. (Hence, in my opinion, this divine correction was not merely about justification by faith but all of the above.)

Also, many mainline Protestant denominations have fallen away from the truth because they embraced the higher critical view that came into vogue in their seminaries in the mid-19th century. This view questioned the validity of biblical authorship, and the plenary inspiration of Scripture. The result is that many of their clergy don't believe in the literal resurrection of Christ and do not preach the true gospel of salvation through faith in Christ alone.

Furthermore, even some evangelical pastors believe that the message of the Bible can change, based on the shifting sands of culture, which is why many have embraced unbiblical views regarding gender, human sexuality, and family.

When a pastor or leader stops trusting the Word of God as their highest authority, they will experience serious decline and/or be removed from their ministries.

2. A leader is not motivated by God's glory

If a leader's primary (subconscious) motivation for ministry is not ultimately the glory of God, they are doing ministry for their own glory. God will not tolerate this for long; in the end, the severe correction can result in the leader being removed from the scene. God says in Isaiah 42:8 that He will not share His glory with another.

3. A leader's value system is worldly

When a Christian leader needs to continually lavish themselves with opulent gifts, replete with a celebrity lifestyle, they have bought into the world system and need to come back to the simplicity of Christ. Even unbelievers can see through the superficiality of these worldly leaders—and it becomes a stumbling block for the gospel. I believe God wants to prosper His people, but I also believe people can go too far and become more fascinated by the temporal than the eternal. God is not going to tolerate this much longer (1 John 2:15-17).

4. Leaders who stop earnestly seeking God

In Acts 6, we see the apostles of the church confronted with a serious issue that could have consumed all their time. Peter's answer was that they were not going to neglect the ministry of the Word and prayer to wait on tables. Their desire to keep first things first was one reason why the early church was so powerful! When leaders stop seeking God, they are no longer infused by His grace to function. They operate in their own strength. Thus, they set themselves up for burnout and moral failure.

5. Leaders stop taking a biblical stand regarding morality

When leaders are afraid to take a public stand regarding ethics and biblical morality, they do not understand the nature of conversion and the gospel. Jesus said we would know a tree by its fruit (Matthew 12:33 and Galatians 5:19-21).

The gospel produces root changes in the human heart that are manifest in lifestyle changes. Thus, the Word of God gives us biblical examples of actions that either correspond or do not correspond with biblical behavior. Hence, human behavior, lifestyle, and actions are a major indicator demonstrating authentic conversion. When pastors and leaders just preach grace and never mention sinful behavior, then they will not see many true conversions. After all, the word "conversion" connotes a change from one particular state to a radically different state of being and living.

Consequently, God will eventually remove the candlestick of a compromising church. Revelation 2:7 details the removal of a candlestick.

6. Leaders neglect their interior lives

When leaders are too busy to reflect, pray, write, meditate, and assess their emotional and spiritual state, they are a potential train wreck. A leader who neglects their soul is a leader who will not last long in this intense climate of spiritual warfare!

God desires truth in our inner man. Mere outward conformity to morality is only behavior modification (Psalm 51 and Matthew 23).

7. A leader searches for significance

Many leaders are driven by ambition, not led by the Holy Spirit. Hence, they get their ministries involved in costly endeavors that God never told them to do! For example, if the economy suffers another huge drop in the future, many church leaders are in so much debt from huge building projects that they may have to sell their properties to survive. This search for significance leads to the sin of presumption. The more I grow in Christ, the more I discover that my longing to feel significant can only be satisfied in the only significant One, Jesus Christ.

Living with contentment is not a popular message today among those on the motivational Christian speaking circuit, but it is one of the most important and basic commands of Scripture. Passages such as 1 Thessalonians 4:11, 1 Timothy 2:2, and Philippians 4:12 teach us to live a godly and quiet life as believers—what some motivational speakers may interpret as a dull, ordinary life.

Christ-centered contentment (not fleshly complacency) in a believer is a sure sign that their sense of significance comes from above and not from the earth. God will eventually humble leaders whose search for personal significance dominates their lives.

Before concluding this section on leadership problems, I want to address one that has its roots in personal leadership struggles that can spread throughout a church, organization, or political system. While the following is the shortest chapter in the book, it still carries considerable significance.

CHAPTER 20

THE SEVEN DYSFUNCTIONS OF AN ORGANIZATION

THE GENESIS FOR THIS chapter came from a *New York Daily News* article that detailed an elected official's failed leadership style, which resulted in chaos and an organizational mess in this official's administration. The official ordered this stunning, confidential report for the purpose of analyzing their operational efficiency when they were serving as a political leader in the metropolitan New York's Tri-State region.

The following seven points are not meant to be a political analysis, but rather a summary of common dysfunctions in all failing systems and organizations, be they businesses, churches, or even families.

1. There is no unifying, overarching vision

When each department functions separately with a lack of inter-departmental communication, there is no real message, no real platform, and no real agenda.

To rectify this fragmentation of information, every department within any organization needs to have one unifying vision they look toward in their work—a powerful vision motivates them. The reason is simple: each piece of the puzzle needs to know how to come together to form the corporate picture or identity. For example, if there is a church in which the Sunday school, worship team, pastoral team, and women's committee all have separate calendars, agendas, and visions, then the church will experience division, even if there isn't any squabbling or overtly divisive talk.

2. There is no communication between the staff and departments

Every successful organization needs to have one unifying calendar and the ability to quickly facilitate events and dates within the departments and staff of the organization.

Systems communication becomes more essential the larger the organization. This is vital; organizations need to continually review their effectiveness in this area, especially as they grow.

Expansion of services without a commensurate expansion of communication will eventually lead to lack of follow-through in delivery mechanisms. This then leads to decreased quality in products or services and a decline in organizational effectiveness and influence.

3. There are people with titles who have no function (When people have titles with no meaning attached to them)

Every organization, including churches, is tempted to reward unqualified people who have been loyal to the organization with important titles. This is a huge mistake, because titles without function mislead people and cause those expecting a service to accompany a title to experience letdown.

4. Leading by consensus and public opinion instead of leading by conviction (When a leader has difficulty in saying "No" to the demands of other people)

This is when an organization has a restaurant's "maître d' style" of management, one which capitulates to the needs and qualms of one's confidence. 1 Samuel 15 teaches this was the downfall of King Saul of Israel: he would always acquiesce to the demands of the multitude because he feared the people.

5. People are being paid to do nothing (When people are put into jobs because of political connections)

There are organizations and churches that hire people because they are related to them biologically or are good friends. Leaders need to be good stewards of the finances of their organizations, which should include regular reviews of all staff members so they are held accountable to perform at the highest levels of excellence possible.

6. The leader plays the staff against one another

Sometimes insecure leaders pit leaders and/or paid staff against one another so that each person's loyalty is directed totally to them. As a result, there are never unified voices among secondary leadership who can threaten their power. Leaders who operate like this violate the biblical law of unity, which is absolutely necessary to obtain a corporate and organizational blessing (Psalm 133).

7. Lack of ability to keep confidentiality

Any organization or church that is going to be successful must have staff that keeps conversations at work, job performance records, and financial records confidential unless otherwise indicated or demanded by a legal investigation.

If there is no trust between the staff and leadership, then there will be a breakdown in the all-important relational dynamics needed for powerful corporate synergy.

I realize by the end of this section you may be feeling depressed or upset, as if leadership challenges are so daunting that no one person could ever hope to meet them. That's why I saved the best for last: guidelines to help pastors and other leaders avoid leadership snarls, withstand attacks, and follow the principles that will enable them to persevere to the very end.

PART III: GUIDELINES FOR THE LONG HAUL

CHAPTER 21

THE SINS AND TEMPTATIONS OF YOUNG, MIDDLE-AGED, AND OLD LEADERS

As I have already pointed out, ministry comes with a host of challenges. One way to meet them head-on is developing an awareness of the sins and temptations that accompany any leadership position.

In my many years of serving in church-related ministry, I have been through various stages of growth and development in ministry and character. Based on self-reflections and observations from years of ministering to, and with, pastors and leaders in the church, in this chapter I will discuss the specific sins and temptations most of us go through based on our age and level of experience.

The Sins and Temptations of Young Leaders (20 to 30 years old)

Young leaders tend to focus more on their gifts, abilities, and accomplishments because they are still trying to find their way. They have great vision, passion, and ambition to accomplish great things for God. While in this stage, they have a lot of energy, are very mission-minded, and want to take the world for Christ. However, although all of the above are very good, they can also be harmful if young leaders are not being mentored by older, wiser, and more experienced leaders.

One of the sins of young leaders is presumption; they run ahead of God because they have zeal without knowledge (Romans 10:2). They tend to build the foundation of their lives more on their gifting and anointing than character development. This can bring short-term success, but failure in the long run when they can't handle the pressure that a lot of responsibility and constant crisis management brings. Thus, their great temptation is to move forward with grandiose ministerial plans without the proper counsel, or hearing from the Lord.

Another temptation is for young leaders to build their ministries on their gifts rather than on godly character, as well as focusing only on their immediate accomplishments without understanding the long-term ramifications.

Other young leaders, especially many of the ones emerging today that are more left-brain driven (the creative class that is driving the entrepreneurial economy), also face a great temptation of jumping from church to church, and/or not being committed to the local church. This is all because as "free spirits" they have an individualistic mindset and no concept of expressing their vision, purpose, and gifts through a corporate body. I have known many talented young leaders over the past several decades who never maximized their purpose because they never stayed planted in a local church. Thus, they wasted their great gifts and spent years being frustrated as they tried to fulfill their vision with much wasted energy, even as a dog exerts a lot of energy chasing its tail.

Corporately, young churches can also go through the same initial phase in their development by focusing more on doing *for God*, rather than hearing *from God* before doing for God. This can lead them into all sorts of trouble because of the sin of presumption, which is often driven by ungodly ambition and competition with other churches in the region.

The key for all of us is to never be lacking in the zeal and passion we had in our youth, while at the same time going through the process of much prayer, fasting, and hearing from God before we attempt huge, time-consuming, debt-producing projects.

The Sins and Temptations of Middle-Aged Leaders (40 to 60 years old)

Middle-aged leaders who have had some success in their youth have the advantage of hindsight and the experience that comes with age. They can have a very balanced approach to life and ministry.

On the other hand, I have observed middle-aged leaders who have had some semblance of success in life and ministry. As a result, the financial affluence they have accumulated and/or progressed to often leads to the sins of complacency and narcissism, with their primary focus going from accomplishments to resting on their laurels. They say to themselves that they have already paid the price and worked hard for many years in the ministry. Thus, it is now "their time" to take for themselves; they have given out their whole Christian lives to others. Now it is time for them to enjoy life, take a lot of time off for themselves, and put their ministry on cruise control.

"Let other people work hard in the ministry," they think, reasoning that they have already paid the price. Because of their seniority, they believe they deserve a high place in the church because they were faithful—sort of like having a "union" or "entitlement" mentality. Thus, their sins are narcissism and indifference as they emotionally detach themselves from the Great Commission of Christ and enjoy the fruits of their labor, because they have enough money coming in on which they can coast.

Corporately, churches can also go from an outreach and missions focus in their beginning stages to becoming more and more self-focused as their priorities change with an aging leadership base.

The Sins and Temptations of Old Leaders (60+ years old)

Old leaders should be at peace with themselves, walking in the joy of the Lord as they shift from individual accomplishments to focusing on mentoring and releasing the next generation to do great things for God!

Unfortunately, in my opinion most leaders do not end well. Many of them become cynical and critical of others as a way of justifying their failure to pursue and accomplish the ministries that the Lord has given them to fulfill. Hence, many older leaders are still immature emotionally. They are in competition with younger leaders in regard to proving themselves and accomplishing great things, instead of gracefully transitioning to the mentoring/parenting stage of their lives. In this stage, instead of being in the front lines of the battle as generals, they should be working behind the scenes as the patriarchs of the move of God—counseling, discipling, shepherding, and encouraging the next generation of generals who have the energy, passion, and calling to lead!

Since many have not gracefully transitioned from the young to middle-age stage, many middle-agers slack off and enjoy their newfound affluence. They don't realize until they are older that they never totally fulfilled the stewardship of the gospel they were entrusted with. Instead of repenting and facing the lost time of middle age, they put everyone else down because they can't face the pain of missing God!

Because of this, I have never been able to invite some older, seasoned leaders to minister in our local church. Once I got to know them, I detected much frustration, cynicism, and a critical spirit because of hope deferred and many unresolved issues.

Corporately older, more established churches should have a vision to give birth to other churches and become apostolic churches that edify and become a resource to smaller or younger churches that need a mother church to guide, protect, and support them. Older churches that are self-centered and self-focused on survival are in danger of missing their greatest calling: reproducing other great churches and ministries.

At this point, I will turn to lessons we can learn from one of recent history's most well-known and tragic figures from the world of entertainment. Although he passed away June 25th, 2009, he remains in the headlines today because of a recently released documentary, *Leaving Neverland*. In addition, his once-proud Neverland Ranch has fallen into neglect and is now on the market, listed at less than a third of its original asking price.

CHAPTER 22

WHAT WE CAN LEARN FROM MICHAEL JACKSON'S TRAGEDY

Note: for a view of this tragedy from someone close to Jackson, read "The Tragic End of Michael Jackson" by Rabbi Shmuley Boteach, The Huffington Post, *7/27/09*

It's a story that will likely live for years to come, even though Michael Jackson died in June of 2009. As the tragic events surrounding Michael Jackson's death unfolded, we found that it was primarily related to the tragic events of his life, starting with his childhood.

Jackson still has many ardent defenders, and some will criticize me for speaking ill of the dead. Yet his story offers the kind of lessons leaders should not ignore. As we look

Poisonous Power

back, we can see that many child stars eventually led tragic adult lives and/or had careers that began to go downhill as they grew older. In these instances, I blame their parents for pursuing fame and fortune for their children at the expense of their emotional health.

Regarding the church, often people launch out into public ministry platforms while they are still emotional infants and not ready for "prime time." It was obvious from the autopsy report that Michael Jackson died (emotionally) years ago, using drugs to deaden the pain of his miserable existence.

Based on my opinion and observations, the following is what leaders can learn from the emotional dysfunction of Michael Jackson.

1. He lived a duplicitous life

Jackson attempted to carry a public persona of happiness, power, and having his life all together, while at the same time battling with inner demons that resulted in him paying millions to the parents of a child who accused him of molestation. During one trial, it was reported that he went to bed regularly with little boys who were staying at Neverland Ranch.

Because of their money and power, men like Jackson often think they can live any way they desire because of an entitlement mentality. There are many ministers and others with public acclaim and esteem who develop this kind of mentality, which mitigates against them seeing the need to fully deal with their inner demons.

2. He had the need to perform to feel loved and accepted

Jackson had the need to constantly entertain to fill a vast vacuum regarding his need to feel loved and accepted. He made the mistake of equating the adulation and applause of fans for love and acceptance.

Many ministers with a vacuous condition in their emotional lives also attempt to perform at high levels as they build large churches and great ministries. This stems more from the drive to feel good about themselves and earn acceptance from others than a leading of the Lord. Thus, they are driven by emotional need, not led by the Holy Spirit. Often what they have in common with Jackson is a lack of parental affirmation, especially from their fathers.

3. He centered his life on his gifts and abilities instead of solid core values

The Jackson parents started a trend early in his life that continued as a pattern in Jackson's life. His incredible talents and abilities drove everything in his life.

Ministers, athletes, political leaders, and anyone who centers their lives in this manner will not leave a healthy legacy, even if their careers start off with a bang! If Jackson's parents would have centered their family life on spiritual values and principles, then they would have made sure their children's exposure to the public was only commensurate to their emotional maturity and ability to stay grounded in their core values.

Often we see great preachers, with amazing ministries, who have terrible falls for this same reason. They attempt to get by with oratorical ability and/or leadership skills and are not grounded in the fear of the Lord, brokenness, humility, and a lifestyle of seeking God.

4. He ran from his pain instead of dealing with it

Jackson, like so many others who have experienced childhood trauma, had to train himself to run from pain instead of dealing with it, since while experiencing it he was too young to understand how to process it. In instances like this, when traumatized youth get older, they become more aware of unresolved issues as their pain surfaces. This triggers a response with two options: get to the root cause of the pain by facing it, or run from it by medicating yourself with mind-altering substances, superficial relational encounters, entertainment, or a centering of your life on tasks and performance. One or more make you feel good about yourself because of your great abilities.

The autopsy of Jackson showed that he had nothing in his stomach except pain-killing pills. Also, his body was filled with needle marks from shooting these drugs. Ministers can also attempt to run from their pain by attempting to utilize the false elixir of superficial relationships, high achievement in work, or entertaining the dark side of adultery, pornography, and lavish living.

5. He constantly lived in the past to recapture what he thought he lost

Often those who have had to grow up faster than their emotional ability to cope regret the loss of their innocence and childhood. Jackson created a fantasy world with Neverland Ranch, replete with an amusement park and a constant influx of young children so he could make up for what he couldn't have as a child. He probably had close relationships with so many children, both because of his compassion for them and also because his emotional immaturity made it difficult to relate maturely with other adults.

Many ministers and leaders also attempt to move forward with their lives without dealing with the many regrets and pain they have tucked deep into their hearts. Sooner or later, we are all compelled to deal with our unresolved past. It will cause a crash if we don't pause to get healed—in the same way you cannot successfully drive a car while looking at the rearview mirror.

6. He didn't keep close friends who held him accountable

Jackson had a close friend, who was a Jewish rabbi, who distanced himself from Jackson because he saw that Jackson really wasn't taking his advice and wasn't willing to change.

Oftentimes leaders will only have around them people who placate them. Those who are serious about growth are those who surround themselves with people who are willing to tell them the truth and confront them. Only those willing to listen to wise counsel will ever be able to maximize their full potential in life.

7. He lived with self-hatred

When Jackson was young, he looked like a black person. As he got older, his skin color and face looked whiter and whiter, to the point that he barely resembled an African-American anymore! (Some think it was a disease affecting his pigmentation, while others think he somehow did it intentionally.) If it involved cosmetic surgery, it showed he was trying to be someone he was not. As he grew older, other aspects of his facial appearance appeared to be altered too. Perhaps the greatest pain Jackson felt was the pain of self-deprecation. For some reason, it seems like he hated himself and, especially after being accused of child molestation, he probably had a hard time really facing who he was.

Every person, including those serving in the ministry, need to face who they are and, when confronted with their sinfulness, go to the cross and allow Christ's blood to cleanse them. Ultimately, we have to accept God's forgiveness for ourselves in spite of our momentous failures in life. Not doing so will lead to our premature demise—in life, relationships, and ministry.

This is why I wrote about Jackson's tragedy. If we fail to resolve deep-seated personal issues, it can ultimately wreck our ministry or leadership position, our personal life, and our dreams. Even when pastors are able to adjust without serious difficulties, unresolved pain can spill into their sermons. When that happens, preaching can hurt others more than it helps.

CHAPTER 23

WAYS PREACHING CAN HURT MORE THAN HELP

THE WORD OF GOD teaches us that the Lord uses the "foolishness" of preaching to save those who believe (1 Corinthians 1:21) and that God reveals His will regarding eternal life through preaching (Titus 1:4). Hence, we can never overstate the importance of preaching to fulfill the purposes of God on the earth. That being said, I have found there are times we preachers do more harm than good with our messages. The following are some of the ways preaching hurts more than helps believers:

1. When we perpetuate the "false self" instead of confronting it

Much of the preaching today is very similar to the motivational speeches and teachings by folks like Tony Robbins,

Napoleon Hill, and others. They are very encouraging messages that have profound truths regarding human capability, goal setting, and maximizing our potential as human beings.

While there is much truth in these messages, there is one fatal flaw: they assume humans can achieve their full potential and purpose apart from relying on Jesus Christ. In John 15, Jesus says "...Apart from me you can do nothing." These motivational speakers perpetuate a Semi-Pelagian message that almost assumes the goodness of men without taking into consideration original sin!

Unfortunately, the same kind of motivational speeches by Christian preachers who attempt to Christianize their teaching by invoking the name of Christ once in a while are now filling up churches around the world. The end result is that this kind of preaching perpetuates the "false self" that only looks for self-fulfillment, self-preservation, happiness, and the fulfillment of our dreams—all without going to the cross and dying to self!

A preacher who only encourages human potential and the fulfillment of self-centered "dreams" based on our "passions" —without basing it on dying to self and seeking first the Kingdom of God—is doing much harm to their followers. Eventually, all these believers will fall flat on their faces, because God will not allow them to fulfill their divine purpose, based solely on human achievement and effort.

2. When we only preach half-truths

Paul the Apostle said that he was free from the blood of all men because he didn't hesitate to preach the whole counsel of God (Acts 20:27). Preachers do more harm than good when they ignore this admonition and merely preach topical messages based on their passions and expertise.

Consequently, preachers will just feed their congregations messages on faith, grace, holiness, evangelism, inner healing, deliverance, or prosperity. This will cause damage to congregants because every truth has conditions and qualifications; hence, if not balanced by other biblical concepts, it results in the negation of certain other truths.

For example, grace and truth came by Jesus Christ (John 1:18)—not just grace, and not just truth. If we preach truth without grace it is legalism; if we preach grace without truth it is antinomianism (the gospel without biblical law and standards), resulting in hyper-grace. Jesus said that some were in error because they knew not the Scriptures nor the power of God (Matthew 22:29). He is speaking about balance. It is not enough to know the Scriptures; we need to have a great understanding of biblical doctrine. We also need to experience the presence and power of God!

For example, I attended a Bible institute for one year in 1979. It was an anti-charismatic, fundamentalist school with some faculty who studied the Scriptures for three to six hours per day, but admitted struggling to pray five minutes per day. Thus, they taught out of a paradigm tilted greatly towards a soulish Christian experience, bereft of the abiding reality of the Holy Spirit.

God is calling us to preach a balance of faith and works (Read the book of James.), grace and truth, and to pursue a life of loving God with our minds as well as our hearts. One of the only ways to ensure a preacher is feeding the church the whole counsel of God is when they preach book-by-book out of both the Old and New Testaments, so they deal with every major biblical subject. When we only preach topically, we run the risk of only preaching what appeals to us!

3. When we take Scripture out of context

I have studied biblical interpretation for years and have integrated my study with such philosophical giants as Hans-Georg Gadamer and such theological giants as Walter Kaiser,

Jr., among others. Suffice it to say, I am going to focus only on a few basic rules for proper biblical interpretation.

Scripture must interpret Scripture. This is perhaps the most important rule regarding biblical interpretation! Consequently, in order to properly interpret a passage of Scripture we need to read the context of the passage. For example, if a passage is teaching a particular doctrine—such as the first coming of Christ—then we need to have an understanding of all the possible Christological passages of Scripture, beginning with the book of Genesis, in order to have a balanced and mature understanding of the purpose and coming of Christ as written in the New Testament, not just the particular passage we are interpreting.

Preachers can misrepresent the Word of God to their flocks when they isolate a passage and impose their own subjective meaning on the text and preach it to their congregations. Unfortunately, most in the church do not study the Bible seriously on their own and believe everything someone teaches them. In my opinion, before we preach about a passage or a biblical truth we need to read the whole book of the Bible to get a sense of the overall theme. Then, read what appears about that topic or truth in all the other places of Scripture. This way, we can preach out of the meta-narrative of Scripture instead of preaching our subjective opinions.

Although no one can guarantee they understand the exact meaning of a text, we can get very close to the meaning if we do the following:

- Read the context
- Compare scriptural references to this truth with the other references in the Bible
- Attempt to convey the original intent of the biblical author before we try to apply it in principle in our contemporary context

4. When we use preaching to promote our own agenda rather than God's will

No doubt there are occasions when all preachers have been tempted to preach a message based on their ambitions and ego rather than being prompted by the Holy Spirit to preach a *rhema* word from the Lord. When preachers use the Bible or the pulpit to push their own agendas (whether to raise money for a building, to convince the people to go in a certain direction, or for another reason—although God can and does lead us to preach at times on these topics), the bottom line is we had better have a pure witness in our spirit that it is the leading of the Lord and not use the pulpit to manipulate the saints!

We who preach will receive the greater judgment from the Lord (James 3:1-2). Thus, it behooves us to speak the oracles of God (1 Peter 4:11) and not our own agendas. I have been in several services where professional preachers got their congregations all worked up to give finances based on their gift of rhetoric. People gave financially because of emotional hype, not faith in God.

Preaching is not a platform for show, hype, or to fulfill our own agendas; it is a sacred stewardship God entrusts to fivefold ministers (Ephesians 4:11) to mature every person in Christ (Colossians 1:28).

5. When we preach out of frustration, anger, and burnout rather than a divine overflow

Overseeing a church can be one of the hardest things in the world! To be effective, most pastors in North America need knowledge in leadership development and real estate, be a people person and a good speaker, work 60 to 80 hours a week caring for the flock and managing the vision, as well as deal with financial challenges, betrayal, family issues, and personal crises of faith and doubt.

Consequently, at times burned-out pastors have gotten up to preach with unresolved issues of anger, hatred, insecurity, resentment, and pain, thus resulting in a mixed message conveying both truth and anger, coming out of a damaged human soul.

I have even witnessed preachers using the pulpit to call out the names of their (perceived) enemies, which amounted to employing a bully pulpit rather than a prophetic pulpit. When preachers do this, they damage their congregations and can even impart to them the same issues of anger, resentment, and wrath, which will pollute their hearers, rather than purify them.

When preachers are filled with anger and/or are experiencing burnout, they need to go away for healing and allow others to minister until they are restored to emotional and spiritual health.

6. When we continually preach out of our limited paradigm and never grow

There are some preachers who stop studying the Word, only stay within their limited circle or denomination, and have been preaching the same pet doctrines for the last 20 to 30 years. Of course, the basic gospel message found in 1 Corinthians 15:1-4 (the *kerygma*) needs to remain the same, but how we apply the gospel to contemporary culture and to our congregations must continually change based on the needs and evolving worldview of the people. Some are preaching today like it is still the 1970s!

As preachers we are called to continually hear from the Lord and, like the sons of Issachar, have an understanding and strategy for the times in which we live (1 Chronicles 12:32). Those who don't grow but preach like they did 20 years ago are answering questions no one is asking and keeping their diminishing congregations isolated and irrelevant.

7. When we preach the ideal without contextualizing it with the real

To expound a bit more on the previous point, I know folks who are teaching their congregations concepts on marriage and family the same way they did 40 years ago. Although the biblical truth remains the same regarding the function and role of family members (Ephesians 5:22-6:4), the times have changed drastically. For example, we cannot preach on Sunday regarding the ideal of marriage and family without being sensitive to the fact that, in many contexts, 75 percent of the people in the audience have come from broken homes and have never experienced the blessings of a nuclear family.

If we just preach the ideal without qualifying our statements it can put deep guilt trips on divorced people and abused spouses and children who have been through hell on earth. They also have to be healed before understanding how to respect their spouses, honor their parents, and learn how to trust other people all over again. Preachers have to understand how to preach both the real and the ideal in order to be effective communicators to their congregations.

8. When we put heavy burdens on people that don't emanate from God

Jesus criticized the Pharisees and religious leaders of His day for putting burdens on the people while not being willing to help lift them (Matthew 23). It is much easier to preach strong messages on the need for prayer, holiness, biblical stewardship, and evangelism than it is to be practical and help process believers into wholeness through biblical discipleship.

Whenever preachers proclaim a truth without explaining the truth and enabling the congregation to have options that can empower them to be disciples, then we can put more guilt than freedom upon the saints. It is far more effective to have things in place for effective discipleship, such as small groups, Bible studies, mentorship, prayer meetings, and retreats. This way, when people are motivated to obey our teachings, there are people in place who will help them walk out these areas of their lives.

9. When we flippantly say, "God said"

Preachers who flippantly use the phrase, "Thus says the Lord," in an attempt to get the church and/or leaders of the church to obey them can do great harm. The challenge comes when the thing we say God told us about does not come to pass, we leave the church and/or God up for ridicule, and we confuse new believers. I have known preachers who have used, "God spoke to me," to manipulate their congregations to get them motivated for a project or to believe for a building—and it never happened the way the preacher said. Either the preacher lied, was deceived by his own desires, or God is confused and can't make up His mind. (I opt for one of the first two.) This causes great chaos in the minds of those who trusted those leaders.

I have learned to rarely say, "God told me." I always preface it by saying, "I believe the Lord is impressing upon my heart." I have learned to test the impressions of my heart by praying with my wife, as well as getting a consensus from all my key leaders before we come out in public and say the Lord is leading us to do a big project or change direction or follow a particular vision.

The book of Jeremiah is filled with examples of God saying He is going to judge the so-called prophets who prophesied from their own minds things that did not come from the mouth of the Lord!

10. When we focus on one people group to the exclusion of other groups

I have been with preachers who have preached to the ethnic majority of their churches and made people of every other ethnic group feel uncomfortable. I have even been in services where they spoke against my ethnicity and said something like, "With all due respect to you and your kind," from the pulpit. There have been folks who have left certain churches because they catered only to the young, the old, the rich, the singles, the poor, or another special-interest group.

Although God has given each congregation and preacher a different field and people to focus on, we need to minister in a way that represents God's heart to all people. God is not Anglo-centric, Afro-centric, Sino-centric, Indo-centric or Hispano-centric. God is not only the God of the poor, but also of the wealthy. God is concerned with both the old and the young and so loved the world (John 3:16)!

Some preachers have also wrapped the gospel around their particular political party or nation and preach as if only the United States (or their nation) is destined by God to bless the world. The blessing will come from the seed of Abraham—not any one particular nation (Genesis 3:15; 12:1-3; 17:5-7; and Galatians 3:29).

Those who intentionally preach an ethno-centric gospel to the exclusion of other human beings impart to their congregations their own biases rather than the heart of God for all people.

11. When we are merely echoes and not a voice

Many preachers are so busy with activity that they have to get their sermons online from other preachers. In violation of Acts 6:2-40, I have known several pastors who merely copy and paste the words and commentaries of other preachers and never receive a word from the Lord regarding what He is saying to their church. Furthermore, this technological (information) age is tempting those of us who preach to depend on Bible software breakthroughs (Logos, Bible Hub and others) rather than the Holy Spirit. The result is that we have great rhetoric without anointing; we have great words without great unction, concepts without conviction, and crowds without disciples!

I have known several great communicators who spend little time seeking the face of God. Even though they preach great messages, there is something missing. They are merely echoes of other preachers instead of speaking as a prophetic voice from the throne of God! In these troubling days our congregation is going to need more than great oratory, historical information, witty quotes, and video presentations. They need to hear what the Spirit is saying to the church in order to thrive in this culture which is saturated by secularism.

Biblical teachers need to be grounded in Scripture so that in their messages they are communicating the counsel of God and guarding against the deleterious practices mentioned in this chapter. Next we want to deal with some of the hazardous habits of executive leaders.

CHAPTER 24

THE CHALLENGES AWAITING EXECUTIVE LEVEL LEADERS

Though many may be associates of either senior pastors or business owners, it is virtually impossible to understand the pressures, sacrifices, and weight of responsibility that rests on the shoulders of effective senior leaders, whether in the church or business world. In the first part of this chapter, I will review some of the hazards of executive level leadership.

1. Executive level leaders often isolate themselves

Many do not speak to other senior leaders because they want to maintain an air of success and respect among their peers. Many do not confide in their associates or staff when they struggle because they are afraid that familiarity will breed contempt.

The Bible teaches us in Genesis 2 that it is not good that man should be alone. Man was made to be in community with others, whether it be family, friends, or vocational colleagues. No matter what the situation, executive level leaders must find others of their ilk to confide in and receive counsel and support from for the sake of the longevity and success of their lives, families, and organizations.

2. Executive level leaders often violate principles of Sabbath rest

Many continually carry the weight and responsibility of their work with them 24/7, even when they are on vacation or with their family during downtime. The human mind can only take so much and must have a total break from stress if it is going to function at an optimum level. It is foolish to try to function at an optimum level with a tired mind and hurting soul. Many do not take a day off each week and attempt to continually function at a high level without breaks to recover and revitalize. This would be as foolish as running a one-week marathon without ever stopping to sleep or eat.

3. Executive level leaders often do not celebrate the processes of success

Often, they are so driven by the long-term product that they do not take adequate satisfaction in the small victories needed to achieve long-term success. In many ways, God considers the process just as important as the product! Because of this, they are continually unhappy, stressed out, and not able to adequately rest because their lack of fulfillment or satisfaction in achieving small victories in short-term goals makes them feel restless.

4. Executive level leaders often judge themselves by the success stories of other leaders

In the same way everyone has a different fingerprint, we all have unique callings and ways to accomplish them that differ from everyone else on the planet. Because of this, we all have different ways to judge success and failure. Ultimately, God will judge us by our faithfulness to our particular assignment.

When we attempt to value ourselves based on the most successful models of leadership in our genre of work, we can do damage to our emotions because we will never come up to the level of every model showcased. The moment we think we have come to one person's level, another person will arise who will have an even more impressive model. That will again cause us to go into an emotional funk and devalue ourselves.

5. Executive level leaders often sacrifice the health of their soul for the urgent matters of pending tasks

I have met numerous high-level leaders who never take time to adequately pray, study, or exercise because of urgent pending tasks in front of them. While there may be seasons for this kind of regimen, neglecting self-renewal and health should be the exception to the rule, which happens only occasionally—and for a very good reason. Never continually sacrifice something that is vital for something that is urgent.

6. Executive level leaders often do not have a plan for personal growth and development

Although most successful executive level leaders know how to work off of a strategic business plan and budget, most cannot say the same regarding a personal plan for their own growth. The ones who can have made the connection that an organization will only grow as far as the executive leader grows. Thus, if they really care about their church or business, they would put themselves on a strict, systematic regimen of reading quality books, listening to quality audio teachings, and having regular conversations with great leaders and achievers.

7. Executive level leaders often put the work of the organization before the health of their family and key personnel

According to Genesis 1:27-28, the foundational principle of subduing the earth and having dominion is not based on achievement in work but on proper male-female relationships (especially in marriage) and having children's children who are properly trained to consecrate the earth ("replenish" in Genesis 1:28 means *to consecrate*). Many high-level leaders get shot down or are stunted in reaching their potential because of marital and family problems arising from neglect. For long-term effectiveness, executive level leaders must learn to prioritize their marriages, families, and the key staff assigned to them to fulfill the dominion mandate in Scripture.

In addition to avoiding these hazardous habits, functioning as an executive level leader means appreciating the reality that you will face challenges to your leadership. In the second part of this chapter, I will chronicle six of the leading sources.

1. Senior executive leaders see the whole picture; secondary leaders and staff see the picture in fragments

Often people don't understand why executive leaders make certain decisions, because they are viewing the situation from their own narrow perspective and realm of influence while the senior leader sees everything from "30,000 feet." Often, people are looking out only for their department or ministry (such as Sunday school, youth ministry, family ministry, or the workers on the assembly line in a factory) because doing so protects their interests. Meanwhile, the senior leader has to exercise leadership based on the whole picture of the puzzle, not just the individual pieces.

2. Senior executive leaders push people to higher standards; secondary leaders and members often empathize with people the leader is challenging or stretching

Often the executive leader is viewed as the "bad guy" because they are in front, leading the charge and pushing staff and members of the organization to new levels of excellence and out of their "comfort zones."

In this scenario, it is easy for secondary leaders who don't have the pressure of making the hard executive decisions to come alongside those being challenged by the senior leader and be the "good guys." This can result in schism and character assassinations against the senior leader.

One of the worst things that can happen is a secondary leader walking in an "Absalom spirit" and stealing the hearts of the people by hearing their hurts and telling them that the senior leader doesn't want to take the time to listen to their gripes or heal their wounds (2 Samuel 15:1-6).

3. Senior executive leaders put the good of the organization before individuals

Unfortunately, there are times a staff member has to be fired because of incompetence or ethical breaches in conduct detrimental to the organization. When this happens, the senior executive leader can be viewed in a negative way by the rest of the staff or members. It is easy for a staff person to think more about the needs of the person fired because they are also serving in a similar staff position, whereas the executive leader has the stewardship from God to look at the good of the whole. In the same manner Jesus sacrificed Himself for the sake of the church, we are never to sacrifice the whole body or organization for the sake of the needs of one person. For example, in our society we see unions put the needs of the individual workers or professional athletes before the needs of a company or team, often to the detriment of all involved.

4. Senior executive leaders are targets of those wanting their position

Often there are people, especially some in secondary leadership positions, who desire to be the senior leader. As a result, their desire for the number one position in the organization leads to envy and jealousy, which then leads them to be involved in character assassination behind the scenes. These secondary leaders want the glory, the glamour, and the gold, but not the incredible stress, sacrifice, and responsibility it takes to serve as the senior leader. No matter how many years a person serves as a vice president or assistant pastor, they are never fully prepared for being the CEO, or the president of a nation, or the leader of an organization!

5. Senior executive leaders are often misunderstood

Because of time constraints and emergencies, senior leaders often have to make quick decisions before having time to go to a committee to build consensus. Built into every effective organization or church protocol must be certain powers vested in the executive leader to make quick decisions because of "executive privilege."

One of the things that made Winston Churchill so great was his ability to make hard and fast decisions during World War II without always depending on committees and bureaucracies.

Although I believe in working through big decisions with leadership teams and committees, there are times when emergencies or unforeseen situations come up that demand quick decisions. During these times, the senior executive leader can be vulnerable to accusations by the members or secondary leaders for violating process, or for having a "top-down" approach to leadership. This is why it is important that an organization have in its by-laws or corporate minutes the power of the executive leader to lead with executive privilege in certain unforeseen situations. With the proper planning and commitment of the leadership teams, these situations can become few and far between to mitigate against this top-down approach. Still, there are certain seasons in which the executive must be way out in front, leading the charge and making the tough decisions the organization needs to thrive in the midst of great changes and challenges.

6. Senior executive leaders are the biggest targets in spiritual warfare

There is a principle in Scripture in Zechariah 13:7, in which the shepherd is struck down so that the sheep scatter. There is real spiritual warfare on the earth, and the main target is always

The Challenges Awaiting Executive Level Leaders

the executive senior leaders and presidents of nations, organizations, and churches. This is because executive senior leaders have the most influence—for good or bad, so when they are attacked by the enemy and fall there is the potential to take down the whole organization or congregation.

It is for this reason people need to lift up their senior executive leaders (CEOs, pastors, presidents of nations) in prayer on a continual basis, so the rest of us can lead effective lives by following those in authority over us (1 Timothy 2:1-3).

As you tackle the many pressures and responsibilities of executive level leadership, don't allow them to distract you from the key issues of life—those things that will mean so much when you reach the end of a long road.

CHAPTER 25

AVOIDING THE LEADING REGRETS OF AN 80-YEAR-OLD MINISTER

THROUGH THE YEARS, I have been around many older ministers. I have noticed that very few seem satisfied with the way they prioritized their time in regard to their life and ministry. Because of this I often spend my time thinking ahead many years from now, to when I will be near the end of my earthly sojourn, and try to visualize the activities and fruit borne that will give me the most pleasure, based on the Scriptures and my calling. The following are things I want to avoid in the years to come so that I will not live my last days with regret, cynicism, and denial:

1. Sacrificing my spouse and children on the altar of ministry

People come and go in a church, but there is only one guaranteed set of people for which a minister will always be responsible: their spouse and children!

Many leaders are so ambitious they try to build a ministry with folks who may or may not be with them a few years down the road. The spouses of ministers are usually the neediest people I meet in a typical congregation. Statistics show that most wives of senior pastors blame the ministry for their marital difficulties! Do we need to talk about what pictures come to mind when we think of the term, "P. K." (pastor's kid)? The children and spouse of senior pastors often become embittered because the senior pastor's focus is constantly on the needs and vision of the church, to the emotional neglect of the ones he is most responsible for!

2. Putting programs before people

Getting new programs off the ground can often be exciting, since doing so often promises to greatly add to the life and vision of the church. Unfortunately, most of the time the amount of energy and focus needed to properly implement a program takes the energy and focus of the senior pastor away from spending time with the key people he/she is assigned to mentor, develop, and release into their destiny! By the time most pastors realize being that program-based has unnecessarily robbed them of the greatest assets for their church's vision—key committed leaders and emerging leaders—they have already passed their prime and spent their greatest energy.

3. Spending most of my time attempting to nurture the whole church instead of concentrating on potential leaders

Lead pastors are often spending unnecessary time, either lamenting the loss of one of their members or spending many hours with high-maintenance people who usually never mature into high-output, fruit-bearing saints.

I learned a long time ago that Satan would try to wear me out with countless hours counseling someone who really has no interest in changing, but loves my attention because of his or her emotional need for affirmation. Since the late 1980s I have made up my mind that I would build our local church based on the priorities laid out by Paul the Apostle in 2 Timothy 2:2, in which he instructed Timothy to spend his time with people who were like this:

- Faithful
- Able
- Called to teach others

If any one of these three components Paul laid out is missing in a person, a lead pastor should not invest vast amounts of time working with them. (Of course, this is not referring to taking care of our needy family members and those God lays on our heart to aid for a season.) For example, a person may have ability but if they are not faithful, then their character is not commensurate with their gifting and they are a train wreck waiting to happen. Or, a person may be very faithful but does not have much anointing or calling on his or her life to be a leader. Thus, this person should be delegated to one of the small group leaders or lay ministers who can, and should, spend adequate time nurturing this potential leader.

Furthermore, every church has folks in attendance that are either part of the "A" team or "B" team. The "A" team is made up of people totally committed to the discipleship process and vision of the church. The "B" team is made up of those who want to attend church, but do not really want to be discipled and/or do not want a person to hold them accountable for growth. They just want to come to church to fulfill the minimum requirements of their Christian obligations.

Those in the "B" category should never be the priority of the lead pastor's time unless the Lord clearly gives the pastor a leading to focus on them. Of course, at times it is also not obvious who is in which category! Sometimes people respond greatly to the attention of the lead pastor. Some do not think they have much of a calling or ability; meanwhile, all they need is the lead pastor to speak a few words to them, which begins a great acceleration toward their Christian growth.

4. Never befriending young people

During his life, Rev. Billy Graham said one of his regrets was that he never prioritized making friends with younger ministers. He said this in his late 80s, when many of his friends had already gone to be with the Lord. This statement made a great impact on me. By incorporating a strategy to speak into the lives of much younger men than myself, I have now started another mentoring group composed of emerging leaders in their early to late twenties and thirties. My goal is not only to develop great leaders for the Lord, but to have a well-rounded life in which I am surrounded by people half my age—not just those my age.

5. Raising up faithful church members instead of sons and daughters

Years ago a church minister once told me not to get too close to people in my young and growing church because it would create jealousy and division among church members who witnessed my favoritism. Thank God I never agreed with or took his advice! The gospel accounts are replete with Jesus showing favoritism with the 70, then the 12, and then His inner circle of three that He took with Him everywhere He went.

I have many titles in my life: doctor, bishop, pastor, and reverend. But by far the title I appreciate most and believe to be most important is when someone in our church calls me "Dad." God is never called doctor, apostle, bishop or the "great general in the sky." He is called Father because a father (or mother if you are a female) is by far the most important relationship any person could have with other people in a church. (I am not counting husband or wife because you are only supposed to have one of those in a lifetime!) In his twilight years, the Apostle John once said the greatest joy he had on earth was knowing that his children walked in the truth (3 John 4).

A few years ago, I was in a hotel room speaking with two ministers who were at least 20 years older than I was. I asked them two very important questions as part of our very meaningful dialogue. The first question was this: In your opinion, do most ministers end well and, if not, what is the number one reason they do not? I was expecting their first answer, but I was not ready for the other reason they both gave. What surprised me was when they said older ministers they meet are dissatisfied with their lives (Some are even bitter and cynical.) because they have few or no spiritual sons and daughters around them in their latter years.

When we do not prioritize and facilitate meaningful relationships that transcend ministry and membership of a church, we will regret it when we are in our twilight years! Members come and go but sons and daughters remain part of your life for eternity, whether you stay in full-time church ministry or not!

Finally, when all is said and done and you are breathing your last breaths on earth, the only fond memories you will have and the things that will matter most to you will be the key relationships you were responsible for. After all, in eternity we are not going to be able to take beautiful cathedrals, homes, cars, money, or prestige with us—only the people we have won to the Lord. Woe to the person who realizes this when it is too late!

To conclude, avoiding these sources of regret will help produce an authentic leader. Attaining this status should represent one of your primary goals in life.

In the following chapter, we are going to elaborate on what it means to be an authentic leader. Being authentic has to do with being true to yourself as a person and true to the God who created you for His purpose.

CHAPTER 26

SIGNS OF AUTHENTIC LEADERS

OFTEN LEADERS ARE NOT true to themselves or to the call of God in their lives. The following are signs that you have been leading from your true, authentic self and not from false expectations:

1. You have a godly rhythm in your personal life

Authentic leaders pace themselves. They don't overreach regarding their ministry schedules because they are not taking a yoke Jesus never gave them. (Jesus's yoke is easy according to Matthew 11:28-29.) Often, overworked ministers are trying to prove something because of an identity crisis or insecurity. Thus, even when they are doing the work of the Lord, they are not doing it for the Lord!

2. You look for deeper relationships

Authentic leaders not only care about their work, but also about connecting to the hearts of the people they serve. They do not look at people as a way to gain a platform for ministry, but honor them with the love of God, which gives them a heart-to-heart connection.

3. You are not always quick to give your opinion

Authentic leaders have learned through trials that they don't have the answers to all the tough questions in life. They are not "answer men" but view themselves as people traveling on a journey through life's processes and seasons with those they are in community with. They attempt to get into the world and context of a person before they offer quick solutions.

4. Your priorities reflect your core beliefs

Authentic leaders live and preach in public about what they actually practice and believe in private. In addition, they schedule their lives around the things they value as based on the assignment received from above. Inauthentic leaders live outside of their core values because they don't practice what they preach, and/or they are driven to perform tasks to please others, even if they themselves have no calling from God to do so.

5. Your preaching includes the whole counsel of God, not just pet passages

Authentic leaders don't just preach messages about prosperity and blessing, but also include the sufferings of David, Paul, Job, and other great saints who grew the most while being tested. Since we are attempting to live risen lives in a fallen world, there will be setbacks and pain in vocation and relationships. Authentic leaders embrace this reality and reflect it in their preaching and counseling, while inauthentic leaders preach only what gets the most excitement and attracts the biggest crowds. When our motives are to please people and not God, we cannot be true to our calling or ourselves.

6. You have true friends

This last section represents the longest portion of this chapter. I am reviewing these points because, in this day and age

Signs of Authentic Leaders

it is common for many Christian leaders to live lives without any true friends. I even had one high-level leader tell me once that he had no friends, and that he kept people at a distance, never expecting anything from anyone so he would not be disappointed.

This is a very sad commentary on contemporary Christian leadership, since friendship is very important for the social well-being of all individuals, irrespective of the kind of position in which you serve. Close friends are a sign of authentic leaders.

God said in the Garden of Eden at the dawn of creation that "it is not good that the man should be alone," which was the impetus for God giving Adam another human being to be his helpmeet and wife (Genesis 2:18-25). Not even all the animals in the Garden of Eden were enough to give Adam adequate company. Scripture teaches us about the close friendship soon-to-be King David had with King Saul's son, Jonathan (1 Samuel 18:1-5), a friendship David said was even better than the love of a woman (2 Samuel 1:26). Jesus told His closest disciples in John 15:15 that He did not call them servants, but friends, because He had told them what He received from the Father. Abraham was given the highest compliment of all when he was called the "Friend of God" (James 2:23). Proverbs 18:24 says that it is possible to have a "friend that sticks closer than a brother." Although many use this verse to refer to Jesus, I also believe the primary meaning of this passage is God connects us with people by choice, not just with our biological families, which came not by our choice but by physical birth.

I have known numerous leaders with no real friends. There are many reasons for this. For one thing, leaders do not know if they can confide regarding their personal challenges without it coming back one day to bite them! Also, high-level leaders who rarely fellowship with or connect to peers are also concerned that, if they share their heart in a true friendship with someone under their leadership, those they speak to will have less respect for them. One major obstacle is also the time demands related to work or ministry, which are so great many rarely have time to cultivate and nurture ministry relationships in a social setting. Often, the only discretionary time available has to be given to one's spouse and family to compensate for the leader's lack of availability at home. Finally, high-level leaders have been disappointed numerous times by people who only wanted to be their friend so they could receive some kind of favor or benefit. Thus, they don't know if a person who is friendly is merely attempting to curry favor with them because they desire something from them. Unfortunately, the reality is, after doing a true analysis based on the following signs, I can say that many leaders do not have even one true friend! The following are signs that you have a true friendship with someone:

1. You truly "like" being with that person

God doesn't just want to love us; He truly wants to "like" us! If God just loves you, then you are no different than the Pharisees and Sadducees who Jesus died on the cross for—people He never really desired to hang out with, even though He loved them and sacrificed Himself for them. In the same way, God has not called us only to labor with people in the ministry for the glory of God, He has also called us to appreciate the gift of friendship—that is, ministering with people we truly "like," not only love! While agape love is God's divine unconditional love, friendship is a relationship based on sharing reciprocal feelings of camaraderie, emotions, kingdom purpose, and social renewal.

2. You confide in that person

It is essential that every human being have people they can share their personal struggles with, sharing information about situations that can truly be used to damage you if that person broke confidence and disclosed your information to others. In spite of the risk, I don't believe God wants a leader to live his or her life with high-level stress and struggles without having a person to bounce things off of for wisdom and encouragement.

3. You miss that person when you are not with them regularly

People in true friendships develop healthy "soul ties" in which their emotions need regular connection. (In the same way your body needs food and your spirit needs spiritual renewal, our emotions crave fellowship with true friends.)

4. You regularly communicate with that person

Those you have a true friendship with will regularly reach out to you via email, text messaging, phone calls, or visits. If you can go months without speaking to a person, then they are not really your friend, just a useful acquaintance. Any person who doesn't attempt to have regular communication with you or regularly avoids contact with you is not really your friend.

5. You have a heart-to-heart connection with that person

Friendship is not just about ministering to a person or working with a person. It has to do with a heart-to-heart connection that transcends work, words, and activity together. It is enjoying an intuitive sense about what a person thinks, what they would say, like, or do in certain situations because you have a heart-to-heart connection. In summary, you really "know" this person. There are not many people who are really in your head and know you as a true friend would.

6. You can depend on that person when needed

A "fair weather friend" is a person who only stays with you in good times, but leaves you in bad times. I have known countless leaders who either morally fell or went through huge struggles in their ministry; most of them told me that their struggles showed them who their true friends were. One national minister who has been in ministry almost 30 years told me (after a personal struggle) a number of times that he "could count his true friends on one hand" because of his experience with people leaving him while he was down and out.

7. This person speaks highly of you when you are not with them

True friends love you so much they try to represent you well before other people, even opening doors for your business and ministry because they want you to succeed in every way. Why? Because your success is truly their success!

When a person I consider a friend never networks me with other key leaders—even when given the opportunity—then I know they are probably not a true friend, but only using me for their own platform.

True friends mutually support, honor, and look out for one another as they help advance our common Kingdom agenda.

8. This person loves you for who you are, not what you can do for them

Those who have the hardest time picking and knowing their true friends are those with celebrity status, or have a lot of money or a lot of power. This is because they never know if a person is relating with them primarily because they are intoxicated with the proximity of celebrity and power. Even though I have a number of tried and true friends who have been with me through many hardships and trials, I know that the sad reality is that if ever my ministry or church ceased to be as successful as it is, or if I resigned from the ministry and became a person without an official title, some of the folks that I presently minister to—and who claim to love me—may forget that I exist!

May all of us be open to allowing God to connect us to the greatest gift a human being can give to another human: the gift of friendship. As you strive to exhibit the signs of an authentic leader, keep in mind there are certain principles for finishing well. That's the subject of the final chapter.

CHAPTER 27

LEADERSHIP PRINCIPLES FOR FINISHING WELL

THERE HAVE BEEN GREAT leadership books on living a significant life and finishing well. (*Halftime* by Bob Buford comes to mind.) I want to conclude this book on a positive note by focusing on how lead pastors and apostolic leaders can finish well.

One of the saddest conversations I ever had was with several older church leaders who confided in me that most leaders they knew didn't finished well. After that experience, I started looking around and having as many conversations as I could with older leaders regarding this subject.

By "finishing well" I am referring to fulfilling the work that God gave us to do (John 17:4) so that we pass into the next world satisfied (Psalm 91:16). Regarding his final days, Paul wrote in 2 Timothy 4:6-8, "For I am already being poured out as a drink offering, and the time of my departure has come. I have fought the good fight, I have finished the race, I have kept the faith. Henceforth there is laid up for me the crown of righteousness, which the Lord, the righteous judge, will award to me on that day, and not only to me but also to all who have loved his appearing."

May all those who read this be able to say these same things!

The following are eight principles that will enable a leader to finish well:

1. You are leaving a legacy of faith, courage, and integrity

In order to finish well, we need to live a life of faith and courage, with no major regrets that we missed the purpose of God because we were afraid to take risks and trust Him. Furthermore, we need to have cultivated lives of integrity without engaging in scandalous behavior that will come back to bite us later in life, thus clouding our legacies. (Joe Paterno's passivity regarding Jerry Sandusky comes to mind.)

2. Adequately equipping the next generation of leaders God sent to you

There is perhaps nothing more important for finishing well than to take aside key people with leadership potential and pour into them so that you are always reproducing yourself in those with capacity to influence many others. The main agenda of Jesus was to pour into the Twelve Apostles—not the large crowds that gathered to hear Him preach.

Senior leaders who focus on preaching and gathering crowds instead of choosing a remnant of people to equip may not finish well because, at the end of the day, you want your disciples to be doing greater works than you before you pass on to the next life. A person will die unsatisfied if they don't see their spiritual children excelling in life and ministry.

3. You successfully transitioned through the four leadership stages in life

There are at least four leadership stages in life. Most leaders never get past the second stage.

The first stage is to be a leader other people can follow. This involves using your gifts to draw a crowd and preach the gospel and create a community of people who follow Jesus.

The second stage is to develop leaders who can produce other leaders. Unfortunately, most leaders only barely scratch the surface regarding this stage because they want to be the ones doing all the preaching, praying, weddings, funerals, and hospital visitations; they need to feel needed. But, those who don't enter this second stage have violated 2 Timothy 2:2, which teaches that we need to focus on developing those few people who are able to teach others.

The third stage is to allow those leaders you have developed to lead so they can develop their own leaders while you focus on coaching the leaders of leaders. This usually happens when a person reaches midlife, with more than two decades of leadership experience. (Each stage can take almost a decade to move into!)

The fourth and final stage, during the final two to three decades of life, is to only concentrate on being a mentor to leaders who oversee networks and movements, and leaders who oversee leaders of leaders. Very few reach this last stage; it may also be true that only a few leaders are even called to reach this fourth stage of leadership. Those called to transition into this stage will not be satisfied in their final days on the earth if they have not walked in this level. (What may be considered successful to some leaders may not be for others called to higher levels of leadership.)

4. You are surrounded by spiritual sons and daughters who carry your DNA

At the end of the day, the crowds come and go, but those you have nurtured as spiritual sons and daughters will always be devoted to you. Perhaps the greatest regret of some senior leaders is that they did not adequately parent the children God gave them, resulting in them having no spiritual children in their later years.

Some older ministers have even said their greatest regret was not spending more time with younger ministers because, when they hit their 80s, most—if not all—of their peers were dead and they were left alone with no true friends. In order to finish well, we need to develop and mentor younger leaders who will sow our DNA into the next generation, as well as other leaders their age who have already accomplished great works.

5. You have adequately journaled or written the main life lessons you have learned, in order to pass them on to others

Perhaps one of the things leaders can do to maximize the impact they will have for the future is to journal their life experience so that future leaders can glean from it. For example, the autobiography of Charles Finney, the journals of John Wesley and David Brainerd, and the writings of Jonathan Edwards, Abraham Kuyper, and others have greatly aided in my personal development. I don't know where I would be today if I didn't have their writings that documented their lives. Perhaps they have had more influence through what they documented for future generations than when they were alive!

I believe in order to finish well we need to at least document the major lessons we have learned, and many may also be called to write at least one book that teaches their life message.

Taking 5-10 minutes a day to journal lessons learned or things God spoke to your soul before you go to sleep can be a powerful force for good for your biological and spiritual children, who will be clamoring for your writings after you pass on to the next world.

6. You have loved your spouse and biological children

One of the greatest regrets of older leaders is having lost their families to the world because they neglected them due to the enormity of the work they had. It will be easier to finish well knowing that we loved our spouses and children to the end, lived sacrificially for them, and did our best to lead them into the way of the Kingdom of God.

What good is it if we win the whole world but lose our children to the world? I don't want my children cursing me on my gravesite or refusing to come to my funeral because I left them a bitter taste for God, the church, and myself, and because I lived hypocritically by feigning love for God and people in public while neglecting them in private.

7. You don't carry any grudges

In order to finish well we need to have a clean slate in our hearts towards those we have worked with. We need to have short accounts with others and walk in the principles of Matthew 18:15-17, so that if we have something against our brother or sister we will immediately speak to them and attempt to resolve it instead of talking about them and harboring unforgiveness in our hearts. Leaders who don't walk in the light with other leaders, or those they work with, will carry unresolved issues that can result in bitterness. In order to finish well we can't walk around in bitterness and resentment, blaming other people for our lack of success or fulfillment in life.

We also need to make sure we don't allow other people to control our emotions by their actions but, in spite of what others may say and do to us, we need to forgive them and have clean and pure hearts before God so we can pass into glory in peace. Bitter leaders never finish well; they finish life angry and unsatisfied!

8. You have pointed everyone to Jesus and not to yourself

Finally, finishing well ultimately depends on whether we lived lives to glorify and bring attention to ourselves or to Jesus. The greatest thing someone can say about us at our funeral will be that we loved God and caused others to love God. More important than us being known for our preaching, large organizations, books, or accomplishments is that we inspired our biological families, our church, and our generation to love and know God passionately.

In conclusion, there are many more things that can be written about finishing well. These are just a handful of ideas I have presented, based on my limited experience and narrow perspective. May God help us all finish well!

CONCLUSION

Leadership is one of the greatest grace gifts God has ever bestowed upon humanity. I call it a grace because this is how Scripture defines it (Ephesians 4:7-12).

The thesis of this book is not to be taken as a sign I am not supportive of leaders, but as an expression of my deep and abiding love for leaders. They are the ones God has chosen to lead the charge for His Church under Him for His glory.

Of course, there is no such thing as a perfect leader (We all have faults and foibles!) but we can all strive to be emotionally and spiritually mature leaders.

My greatest prayer for this book is that it will result in many leaders, churches, and organizations using it to help cultivate a healthier, more mature, and Christ-like approach to leadership in both the church and the workplace.

Sincerely,
Joseph Mattera

ABOUT THE AUTHOR

Dr. Joseph Mattera is an internationally-known author, consultant, and theologian whose mission is to influence leaders who influence culture. He is the founding pastor of Resurrection Church, and leads several organizations, including The U.S. Coalition of Apostolic Leaders and Christ Covenant Coalition. Dr. Mattera is the author of 10 bestselling books, including his latest "The Divided Gospel," and is renown for applying Scripture to contemporary culture. To order his books or to join the many thousands who subscribe to his newsletter go to www.josephmattera.org.

Additional teachings and resources by Dr. Joseph Mattera, can be found at:

Web: *www.josephmattera.org*
Audio: *https://soundcloud.com/josephmattera*

Other books by Joseph Mattera – Available for purchase on Amazon:

Kingdom Revolution
Kingdom Awakening
Ruling In The Gates
Walk In Generational Blessings
Understanding The Wineskin of the Kingdom
An Anthology of Essays on Apostolic Leadership
Essays on Cutting Edge Leadership
Travail to Prevail
25 Truths You Never Heard In Church
The Divided Gospel

Connect with Dr. Joseph Mattera at any of the following locations:

740 40th St.
Brooklyn, NY 11232, USA
718.436.0242 Ext. 13

Facebook:/josephmattera
Twitter:/josephmattera
YouTube:/josephmattera
info@josephmattera.org
Instagram:/joseph_mattera

www.ingramcontent.com/pod-product-compliance
Lightning Source LLC
Chambersburg PA
CBHW071115160426
43196CB00013B/2579